CW00505644

Redesdale *Born on* Recalled *the Hill*

Raymond Taylor

**Memories of a Farmer's son
Growing up at High Leam
West Woodburn
1942 – 1965**

REDESDALE RECALLED

Dedicated to my late Parents
Henry Hugh and Elizabeth Scott Taylor

and my immediate family and their future generations

as a historic basis and reference for

inspirational continuity.

Inspired from reading Jimmy Nail's autobiography 'A Northern Soul' I decided to record my own very different life experiences. I wanted to write about my place of birth and my early developing and teenage years at High Leam, overlooking the village of West Woodburn, in the middle and post War period up to June 1966 when Beryl and I married and began a new life in the West Riding of Yorkshire. My story is intended to serve as a record of my agricultural and family background and an interesting journey through the early part of my life for the benefit of generations to come. These memoirs are narrated in unsophisticated language and are based on the encounters and evolvement of country life in general around that time and true recollections surrounding the first twenty-two and a half years of my life in a rural environment of the North East.

ACKNOWLEDGEMENTS

I wish to convey my sincere thanks and appreciation to all those whose valuable contributions have made this publication possible. In particular, my mother, the late Elizabeth Scott Taylor, for her excellent memory and recall of my early childhood years; my brothers, David and the late Andrew Taylor, for their confirmation of the dates of improvements and important events on the farm; my childhood friend and best man, Brian Wood, for his recollection of our early mischievous antics together; the late Colonel Richard Cross and his wife, who cordially hosted my nostalgic revisit to High Leam in 2009; and Dr. Ian Roberts, learned historian of Redesdale, for his advice in my search for historical information. I must also thank my friends, Dr. Alan Leading, Alan Spree and Peter White, for their painstaking contribution to grammatical corrections, formatting and structuring of my story and, of course, my wife Beryl for her patience and assistance with proof reading and general arrangement. This book, however, would not have reached publication had it not been for the help of Stan Owen and the Heritage Centre, Bellingham, for their support and dedication to editing and final presentation.

In conclusion, I pay tribute to the late Jack and Nancy Wood, who included me in their social activities and introduced me to the wider world, and to my parents, the late Henry Hugh and Elizabeth Scott Taylor, who toiled tirelessly in the face of agricultural adversity to provide a sustained quality of life for their family.

CONTENTS

PART 1　Living at High Leam

My parents, Henry Hugh Taylor and Elizabeth Scott Douglas, married in Chevington parish church on 29th April 1939. My brother Andrew was six weeks old when my parents moved into High Leam on 11th May 1940. On the same day, John (Jack) and Annie (Nancy) Wood moved into the farm cottage. Jack worked for Dad for almost twenty-six years. He was an experienced hill shepherd, the eldest of the three sons and four daughters of Matthew and Ciscilia Wood of Silloans Farm on the Redesdale artillery ranges.

High Leam faces south and is almost 750 feet above sea level with fine views over the picturesque Northumbrian countryside. The 380 acres of hill land was wet and infertile and these unsatisfactory conditions resulted in the loss of livestock and severe hardship in the first year from poor health and disease mainly spread by sheep ticks.

The farm house interior consisted of a back kitchen with a coal-fired water boiler (copper) and a large living kitchen under a wood beamed ceiling. A rise and fall clothes rack was suspended above a black-leaded fireplace with an oven and a stone paved floor.

A massive eight-door cupboard, almost the height of the kitchen, stood the full length of the north wall. This was in two parts and its installation was accomplished by the removal of the front window sections. The top of the cupboard provided a safe and secure place for my Dad to keep his twelve-bore double-barrelled shot gun. There was a separate marble shelved pantry and three reception rooms off a long right-angled passage that led to the front door and steps that were once covered by a rustic entrance arch.

Cold water was supplied in the kitchen by a single pipe through the wall from the adjoining garage and to the back

kitchen over a large ceramic Belfast sink. The long passage also gave way, through a heavy cloth covered and studded door, to a square baluster and wreathed handrail staircase and north-facing round-headed window.

Five high ceiling bedrooms with period decorative deep moulded cornices and a separate chain operated flush toilet closet could be accessed from a large stair landing.

1940 Rustic entrance arch: Mum and Andrew (right), Nancy Wood (middle) and Mum's sister, Ethel Barrass (left)

A further staircase next to the pantry led up to a room over the living kitchen which remained a storage attic. All rooms in the house had Georgian style single-glazed sash windows with hinged wooden lockable panelled shutters and the bedrooms were adorned by open Victorian style fireplaces. High on the wall, behind the door from the living kitchen to the long passage, was a number of metal bells, each connected to wire cords that hung from the ceilings of the five bedrooms. Each bell had its own distinctive chime from which the one-time servants of the house would know exactly which room required their services. Whenever any of us were ill in bed, we used this method to gain Mum's attention.

Jack and Nancy Wood lived in the farm cottage adjoining the farm house, which contained a living kitchen, also with a black-leaded fireplace, an oven and a side boiler, a pantry and an upstairs bedroom. One of the ground floor reception rooms of the farm house was hived off to the cottage for use as a second bedroom. The cottage did not have running water. A cold water supply was provided from an outside tap over a grated gulley adjacent to the nearby riding stable. An outside bucket toilet with wooden seat was situated next to the coalhouse about thirty yards away in the stack yard. So chamber pots were essential to avoid a cold trek outside during the night.

The extensive stone farm buildings with six stone arches for animal housing were in good condition and adequate for farming in the early twentieth century. They provided cow byres with an inbuilt triangular stone dated 1707 opposite the farm house, a cart shed with a tall Roman milestone supporting the roof, stables, pig sties, a calf house, two courtyards, hay lofts, a hay-hole, barns, a huge granary and a five-bay tin roofed Dutch barn hay shed in the stack yard.

PART 2   Early Years 1942-1947

At about 2 am on 15th October 1942, under the medical care of Doctor Kirk from Bellingham, I was born in the front bedroom, located on the west side of the farm house, and lived my life at High Leam until I was twenty-two and a half years of age. My brother Andrew had been born two years earlier.

Jack and Nancy Wood lived next door and helped on the farm. Their only child, Brian John, was born on 13th September 1943. We still share fond memories of our playful years together around the farm at High Leam.

The Second World War was escalating and German prisoners from Otterburn Camp, as well as the local Land Army and evacuees from the vulnerable industrial areas, were used to boost labour on surrounding farms. It was not unusual for the Land Army to make the most of fine summer days by assisting in haymaking until late into the evenings, creating rain-dispelling hay pikes that remained dotted around hayfields across the countryside until finally being transferred to hay sheds or hay stacks by horse-drawn, back-tilting, hand-cranked, wind-on hay bogeys. German prisoners were transported from Otterburn Camp and collected daily, providing an additional work force on the farms. They were energetic workers and Dad, apparently at a loss where to deploy them, suggested they clean out the hen houses, resulting in twenty barrow loads of hen manure being extracted and brought to the front field in one day.

According to my parents, they were polite young men, no different to our own, compelled to fight a war within a foreign country. Mum felt sorry for them, particularly when she saw the disgusting packed lunches they were supplied with from the Camp NAAFI. She provided them with cooked dinners and threw their sandwiches to the pigs. In return, they were loyal and trustworthy and would alert Dad to any extreme Nazi allies amongst them. Dad was an old-fashioned farmer, who always wore a chequered cloth cap, waistcoat and braces, never a belt, and never went on holiday. He had a strange but infectious dry sense of humour and his pet hate was fish in any shape or form.

One of my earliest memories is when I was almost three years old and being taken to hospital with a broken arm. Dad had given Andrew a Shetland pony for Christmas and the Germans wanted to see Brian Wood and me on his pony. But they had failed to tighten the girth belt properly and, as the saddle slipped round, we both fell off, with me falling on to a wooden sledge, suffering a broken right arm and an emergency admission to Hexham General Hospital. Apparently the German prisoners were devastated and couldn't do enough to help. I remember very little else about the war other than that we were all supplied with gas masks, which, I am pleased to say, were never used.

Being over a mile out of the village of West Woodburn and having no other children around, Brian and I made our own entertainment. We were almost inseparable, playing all the usual games that young lads play, such as hide and seek, cowboys and Indians, building dens and playing football. Although Andrew was that bit older than us and joined in some of our mischievous adventures, it was just Brian and me for most of the time. As growing children, Andrew and I had the usual disagreements that young brothers have and occasionally those disagreements developed into conflicting brawls, usually on the way home from school. On the rare occasion that Mum did catch us fighting, she would shout for Dad to bring his stick, which he did, but he never used it. He just told us off and said that we should not be so stupid.

One afternoon, we received a visit from the village bobby, PC Hudspeth, for some reason related to the farm. He lived in the Police House on the left hand side of the A68 going up towards the railway station and, whilst having a cup of tea with my parents, sent Brian and me off to play with his Police helmet, only to find us using it as a bucket to wash his car with water from the horse troughs. We thought we were doing him a good turn but he didn't see it that way.

On another occasion, we caused a fire in the hay shed, which thankfully was almost empty. We had been playing with matches that caused a small fire amongst the left over hay deposits and, when our own biological water supply failed to extinguish the smouldering hay, clouds of smoke, fanned by a westerly wind, became visible as they began drifting across the front field. Naturally this caused such panic and chaos that it sent everyone running with buckets and a stirrup pump to snuff it out, following which we received a strict lecture on the dangers of playing with matches. Much of the time, we played cricket in the yard at the back of the farm house, using an original stone horse-mounting block as the wicket and, much to my Dad's annoyance, the occasional window strike

8

providing proof that a six had been scored; but the vast front lawn was our main playground and football pitch.

Everybody, including visiting friends and relatives and even Nancy Wood with skirt and pinafore tucked into her bloomers, joined in our ball games. Dad had a lucky escape one afternoon as he defended our goal area, with a Woodbine dangling from his bottom lip. To his misfortune, a volley from Brian hit him full in the face producing a vivid colourful display of red sparks and cigarette ash, which my Dad frantically dusted off his face and shirt, with no lasting ill effects. Our annual Guy Fawkes bonfires were held at the bottom of that lawn, where we would all gather and let off lots of fireworks. From there we could see many other bonfires and fireworks across the valley lighting up the evening sky.

The two mothers developed a lifetime friendship as they became the support and backbone to our Dads, who worked that farm until December 1965. As a farmer's wife, dedicated to the success of the business, my Mum, in addition to her household work, took on her own specific tasks around the farm: rearing poultry, milking cows, feeding calves and pigs, making butter, etc., and, along with Nancy Wood, providing help and the necessary food at busy times such as potato picking, pig killing, poultry plucking, haymaking, harvesting and threshing days. She also helped with sick lambs, restoring their fragile lives in front of the open coal fire and gently nursing them back to good health with bottled milk warmed through by stirring it with a red hot poker, as well as hatching out goslings and chickens in the oven, unless we just happened to have a broody hen available.

Mondays were usually wash days that lasted many hours, boiling up water in the back kitchen boiler before transferring it with a copper quart pot to a poss-tub (dolly) and manually dunking and swirling clothes, collected in turn from assorted piles on the floor, until clean. Some light-coloured clothes, particularly with collars and cuffs, had to be scrubbed with Carbolic soap first to remove stubborn stains; then, with purpose-made wooden tongs, the clothes were fed through a hand-cranked mangle with wooden rollers before being hung out to dry on the ceiling pulley rack in the living kitchen or pegged on a wire clothes line in the stack yard, weather permitting. For a time, we used one of those square box-like washing tubs on legs, with a handle on top that you turned to swirl the clothes around, until the arrival of electricity when we got an upright Hotpoint washer with a rubber-roller wringer attachment on top. Ironing was also quite primitive at first, using a box iron with two iron slugs that were alternately swapped from the fire back to keep the box iron hot. We also used a flat iron that was heated over the coal fire in a protective tray and later moved on to a state of the art Calor Gas iron and finally an electric iron.

An alternative method was to fold a clothing item neatly under your mattress, which, when slept on overnight, produced a neatly pressed garment the following morning. With so many routine chores to attend to around the house, it wasn't easy in those early years juggling with all those necessary jobs around the farm and the demands of motherhood, which, at times, meant that we did not have the constant focus and educational encouragement that many children enjoy today and simply just had to make our own entertainment. We grew our own produce and so always had plenty of food and, in fairness, we enjoyed a reasonably satisfying, happy, comfortable and well cared for childhood.

We had very severe winters around that time and the 1947 storm was exceptionally bad. February, with a distinct lack of sunshine, was the coldest February on record in some areas with snow falling in parts of the British Isles on as many as 26 days. Northumberland must have been one of those areas, as the snow was deep, dry and powdery and was soon whipped up into huge drifts by the high winds that followed.

The drifts piled high against buildings and stone walls and buried many sheep that had gathered against them for shelter. Any chances of a hill farm recovery was still aggravated by the shortages of food and fuel that remained after the Second World War and the sudden loss of livestock in the storm was yet another serious setback. Even the rabbits were scratching at the windows searching for food. The snow storm had been less severe in the South of England and the affected farmers in the North were able to apply for a grant from a special fund, set up by Southern farmers, to help replace lost livestock. Most roads were blocked, including our mile-long trek to the village. My Dad dug a path through the snow to get Andrew to school but the storm became even worse as it continued into March and the paths were again filled with drifting snow. Living on a hill was great for tobogganing by us youngsters, but not so much fun pulling the sledge back home. Dad acquired a horse-drawn sledge, which, as the temperatures plummeted and the snow hardened, made it possible to traverse straight over the tops of ditches and stone walls, proving an invaluable implement for delivering fodder to outlying livestock. It was quite a large contraption, similar to a farm cart, but on runners instead of wheels and drawn by chains attached to the horse harness rather than shafts. We once collected Andrew from school in this contraption but, most of the time, the school was closed until about 10th March when warm air from the South created a rapid thaw and severe flooding. Long icicles hung from the farm buildings like huge stalactites and broke off as they melted in the thaw, crashing to the ground like spears. You just had to make sure you were not under them at the time.

Dad was an experienced horseman and would occasionally break-in young horses himself. He had worked with them from being a young man, often getting up at four in the morning to mow hay or plough a field. I remember him lunging a fiery-spirited young Shire horse in the back field and taught it to pull, by harnessing it to a very large heavy log. The horse didn't like it, initially kicking out and scrubbing skin off its thighs against the heavy chains, but soon learned to be more respectful with the log attached. Dad liked his horses and, whilst he had to be forceful with them, ensuring that they knew who was boss, he was never cruel. In fact, we would often find him in the stable, with curry comb and dandy brush in hand, grooming and plaiting their tails. Horses had to be re-shod about every six weeks and this was done on the farm by leather apron-clad Jonnie Ormiston, the blacksmith at Otterburn, later succeeded by his son Robbie. Dad and I visited their house on the day that King George VI was buried in 1952. I remember the date, 15th February, because of the one minute silence that we strictly observed.

PART 3   Schooldays 1947-1953

During the autumn of 1947, at the age of five, I was introduced to West Woodburn County Primary School, attended by about thirty pupils and located in the centre of the village slightly up from the Post Office run by Mary Pigg. Other shops in the village were Jim Charlton's butcher's shop on the corner with the Yellow House Road, Matthew Reay's general store just around the corner and Lizzie Wheatley's confectionary shop on the corner of the road to Bellingham, near the old stone single track hump-back bridge over the river Rede that was replaced with a modern, wider version in 1957. There were two public houses, The Bay Horse, an 18th century Coaching Inn within the village, and the Fox and Hounds at Brandy Bank, opposite Norman Wallace's Garage and Petrol Filling Station. A surgery run by the Doctors from Bellingham was held on selected days in a room in Jean Hamilton's house, within the village, and the cemetery was located at the ancient St. Cuthbert's Church of Norman times at Corsenside, between Dykehead and The Brigg Farm. Funerals commanded more respect then and Dad kept a dark suit and bowler hat for such occasions. I still have the bowler hat as a keepsake in memory of my Dad.

Apart from passing traffic along the A68, West Woodburn remained a quiet parochial little village, well maintained by the parish Council. The roadsides were regularly swept and grass verges mowed by use of a hand-held scythe or sickle or twin-handled 'Allen auto-scythe' grass cutter and the grass raked into small neat piles for later removal. The School was supplied with bottled milk by Willie Telfer of The Park, which, upon his death, was taken over by Billy Brown. In the 1950s, however, school milk was temporarily replaced with flavoured milk tablets. I particularly liked the banana flavour. Apparently that situation arose in areas where the Education Authorities were unable to make satisfactory arrangements for the provision of fresh milk.

The Headmaster and the Deputy at the School were Mr. Frank H. Graham and his wife who lived in the School House. Mr. Graham died suddenly on 5th June 1951 and the position of Head passed to Mrs. Graham who held that post for many more years. During my six years there, I recall her being assisted at different times by a Miss Mitchinson and a Miss Calder. I really enjoyed playing football, rounders and cricket and joined in whenever I could, mostly at playtimes in the concrete school yard, much to the annoyance of Ivy and Tommy Thornton, as our ball frequently went over the wall into their adjoining well-tended garden.

Sometimes, on particularly frosty winter days, we would create an icy slide in the concrete school yard that kept most of the boys occupied at playtime whilst the girls enjoyed skipping and hopscotch. Occasionally, we played football on the White Acres field adjacent to the school, where the school sports days were held and school group photos were taken, around the time the new houses at White Acres were being built. We did manage to field a football team and, having kitted ourselves out with exercise books tucked down our socks for shin pads, played Otterburn School on their home ground but disappointingly lost the match. It was Miss Calder

13

who had decided to reward me and another boy, Gordon Wallace, for some good effort, by taking us out to lunch. Unfortunately, I was ill on the actual day and Gordon had to endure lunch alone with Miss Calder at the Bay Horse. It took him a long time to forgive me for that.

Mrs. Hardie from Hill Crest was the head cook who prepared the school dinners in the kitchen adjoining the smaller of two classrooms that were divided by a large sliding partition. The beginners and younger element occupied the small room whilst the bigger room contained individual wooden desks with inkwells for the older children, a free-standing swivel blackboard, a coke burner, and a piano on which Mrs. Graham accompanied our school assembly hymns. A cloakroom was located at the other end of the school and the boys' toilets were at the bottom of the school yard. The girls' toilets were tucked away behind the school.

What I hated most about Woodburn School was the School Dentist who every so often would park his treatment caravan in the school yard and call us out of class, one by one, for examinations, fillings or extractions. I eventually refused to go and had to be registered with a dentist at Hexham, an upside of which was an extra day off school.

Many of the outlying areas benefited from school transport in the form of an old Alvis shooting brake provided by Norman Wallace. We, however, were not so lucky and the only option was for Andrew, Brian Wood and myself to walk the one-mile journey there and back daily, whatever the weather, though there was a brief short cut that took us from Woodhouse, across a wooden bridge over a burn and along a footpath through Miss Mitford's horse grazing pasture to a metal kissing gate next to the main A68.

Miss Lona Mitford lived at Fellside, a secluded, picturesque country house with stables, where the road descends sharply from the A68 to Woodhouse. She raised fine horses and could often be seen riding them around the village and countryside. She had a nasty fall one day whilst riding through the stack yard at High Leam when she failed to see the wire clothes line and almost decapitated herself. Whilst not badly injured, she was, to say the least, badly shaken.

One of the houses at Woodhouse was occupied by Graham Hedley, a carpenter who undertook the occasional joinery job for my Dad and kept his motorcycle and sidecar in our stone building at the side of the farm road entrance. Another house was occupied by Bob Cragie who often helped out on the farm and would from time to time present my Dad with a section of his home produced honey.

Andrew did quite well at school, gaining his Northern Counties Certificate, but I never much cared for school. Most of my reports ended with the words "could try harder" and there was a quiet expectation that I would do well in the Eleven Plus exams. That wasn't to be and I let everybody down, including myself, and, from that point forward, I never did anything special or achieved any formal qualifications, though I did learn all my times tables perfectly. They were printed on the back of every exercise book so there was no excuse for not learning them. When Andrew was off school for six weeks with Scarlet Fever, I recall wishing it was me, though I did manage some time off with the usual Chicken Pox, Whooping Cough, Mumps and Measles. Brian Wood was the first to get measles and my Mum was keeping us separated to avoid contamination. Dad, however, said I would probably get them anyway and suggested we play together as normal. We did and in a short time I had measles too.

We all benefited from the occasional day off on Election Days when the school was used as a polling station. Arthur Bell would present himself in his Special Constable uniform to ensure full compliance of the Election Rules. Arthur Bell was the local driver of the Blaxter Quarry wagon, which he kept in a lock-up garage half way along the East Woodburn Road.

My Dad's first car was a Morris Ten in which he took me to the village on evening visits to conduct financial business with Mary Pigg at the Post Office, where we had our own Post Office Savings Accounts to invest money realised from bottle-fed pet lambs. As a passenger, you were expected to open and close all those farm gates. Instead of getting in and out of the car every time, it was easier to step on to the running board that all cars had in the 1930s and 1940s and hold on to the side of the car, from gate to gate. Unfortunately, it required an expensive repair after Dad topped it up with *used* engine oil, causing a blockage in a circulation pipe and related friction wear on the crank shaft.

All our orphaned lambs were bottle fed until set on to a new mother and any spare lambs became our very own pets. Ewes that had lost their lambs, for whatever reason, would reject any attempts to become a foster mother to another lamb and many methods were used to trick the mother into believing the lamb was hers. As her identification was usually by smell, a common tactic was to skin her dead lamb, rub it all over and attach it to the orphan, or to put a strong-smelling substance such as whisky on the lamb and on the mother's nose. Sometimes these methods worked and sometimes they didn't but, without doubt, the quicker you set on a new lamb, the stronger the chance of the new mother adopting it. A common disease amongst lambs was Orf, a contagious infection around the mouth similar to impetigo, which, through my contact with lambs, infected me for a short time.

I was still quite young when Dad bought his first tractor, a Standard Fordson, registered number BNL 37, which started on petrol and, when warmed up, could be switched over to a more economical fuel, a type of paraffin called Tractor Vaporising Oil or TVO.

One of the tricks that Brian and I did was to hide some spanners in the radiator of the tractor, which damaged the internal water circulatory fins, necessitating an unnecessary and rather expensive replacement radiator. This tough old machine, however, made light work of the tasks previously undertaken by horses, which were gradually made redundant and phased out.

Times remained difficult as the country struggled to recover from the Second World War and many people were still destitute. From time to time, we would be blessed with the presence of a hungry tramp, who would install himself in one of the cow byres. These tramps were harmless individuals who had nowhere to go and my parents provided them with some food and drink, though Dad's view was not to treat them too well otherwise they would never leave. They usually stayed for a few days before moving on somewhere else.

Dad was still striving to make a healthy living at High Leam when a newly-acquired herd of six Highland 'Kylie' cattle suffered a fatal disease and a new inoculation, used on pregnant ewes, produced swingback in our crop of lambs, many of which had to be slaughtered. On top of that, his Fordson tractor slid out of control and overturned while Jack Wood was spreading slag on the slippery, steep hillside in the second field above Woodhouse. Apparently, Jack had a very lucky escape but the tractor required more extensive and costly repair work.

Tending the large front lawn with an old push lawn mower was demanding work and we eventually bought a 1950 Atco Lightweight 14 inch-cut cylinder lawn mower complete with a rubber-wheeled transport cradle. Power was provided by a Villiers two-stroke 79cc petrol engine. It had a metal coned clutch and a kick start and was a swine to start if the petrol-oil mixture was not to the correct consistency. It later became my responsibility to keep the front lawn tidy and, over the years, I got so attached to that old lawnmower that I kept it and recently restored it to its original working condition.

Granddad Douglas was a regular visitor to the farm. He smoked those old disposable clay pipes and liked shooting rabbits and other vermin that poached any available poultry on the farm. He was a crack shot with a twelve-bore double-barrelled shot gun and often came back with a dead fox or badger. We knew of one badger sett under some tree roots in one of the burns and a fox's den in one of the West Side fields. We could sometimes hear the foxes barking on a warm summer evening and, if we were lucky, we might get a glimpse of a vixen playing above ground with her cubs. Jack Wood's dog Sweep once put up a fox in the front hayfield and chased it until it took refuge in a rabbit hole where only Sweep's hind quarters and frantically wagging tail were visible above the ground. Determined not to allow the fox to escape and raid yet another hen house, Jack pushed some straw into the hole and set fire to it to suffocate the fox. Too much smoke was escaping, so he sealed the entrance by sitting on it and, after a few minutes of singeing his backside, his walking stick detected the limp body of a dead vixen.

Uncle Eric, my Mum's youngest brother, was also a good shot with a shotgun and .22 rifle, though he lost his index finger in a mining accident and had to use his middle finger on the trigger thereafter. He never let that affect his accuracy and it was he who taught me to shoot, using tin cans on a stone wall for target practice and, thanks to him, we enjoyed many a rabbit and pigeon pie. That was, of course, until the first spread of myxomatosis arrived, a fatal disease amongst rabbits, illegally introduced to France in 1952 and reaching the UK the following year. It has always been suspected that the spread of the disease throughout the UK was assisted by farmers, who were glad to see a reduction in these crop destructive pests. We were plagued with moles, which may have poor eyesight but are very crafty, with an acute sense of smell enabling them to detect and avoid any interference in their underground runs. However, we became experts at catching them in traps and would often have a dozen displayed on a barbed wire fence, alongside some dead crows that had fallen victim to Dad's shotgun after overstaying their welcome in a freshly-seeded cornfield.

Dad and I were in the village one evening in the car when I was handed a Border terrier pup by Christopher (Kit) Johnstone, a local character, who lived at Little Ridsdale and kept poultry on The Green by the river off the road to Bellingham. We called the dog Piper. He grew up with a natural roaming instinct, often returning with a stench of dead animals or, as they say in Northumberland, had been eating 'kett' and once with his backside peppered with shotgun pellets, no doubt from a local protective livestock owner. Until 1987, pet dogs over six months old required dog licences, whilst working dogs had exemptions, which were all checked periodically by the Police. Piper's licence had expired and, when Dad learned that the Police were about to visit, he hid the dog next door, invited the Officer inside for a cup of tea and told him "The damned thing died." Piper was eventually replaced with a Border terrier bitch called Judy.

Festive Occasions

Whatever difficulties our parents were experiencing, we were always well provided for. Birthdays were always celebrated with friends as we tucked into a special tea party of mainly homemade delicious food, which included fresh scones containing coins wrapped in greaseproof paper. The problem with that was in our attempt to find some higher value coins we ended up full of scones. Perhaps that was the idea. Christmas was a very special occasion with a heavily decorated pine tree in the kitchen, lots of balloons and streamers, berried holly, mixed nuts, fruit and sweets strategically placed in the first sitting room, in which we would gather for such occasions; and, as that famous Christmas song goes, chestnuts roasting on an open fire. There was a fine balance between roasting them sufficiently to get the shell to peel off and leaving them too long when they would explode. All these special arrangements, ingredients and aromas have left me with a distinct nostalgic and memorable reminiscence of Christmas that was always preceded by a long day shopping in Newcastle. I can recollect how Brian and I, as small boys, were trailed around Fenwicks, Binns and many other departmental stores in Northumberland Street and being fascinated by the complex pneumatic tube networks that whizzed cash away at record breaking speed from the pay desks to the cashier's office. The day usually ended with a visit to Santa's Grotto before returning to the bus station in the Haymarket, late in the afternoon, to catch the bus to Bellingham where Dad would meet us.

Andrew and I were always up early on Christmas morning and received Christmas stockings and many presents from our parents, friends and relatives (never failing to get an annual copy of Black Beauty from someone). One year, Brian and I each got a genuine willow cricket bat which we were advised would last longer if we smeared them regularly with linseed oil.

Andrew, Brian Wood and Raymond

The oil made the wood less brittle but they were still not strong enough to withstand the introduction of harder cork and leather cricket balls and eventually succumbed to our treatment. We later enjoyed a huge 'fresh off the farm' 25lb turkey lunch with homemade bread and onion stuffing, prepared by Mum at twelve o'clock on the dot, as was normal routine on the farm at that time. Work never ceased, even on Sundays, but this was the one special day of the year when only the necessary tasks were attended to, such as feeding, milking and mucking out livestock, and my Dad enjoyed the remainder of the day with his family. It seemed no time at all since we had finished off the turkey remains when it was New Year's Day and, whilst it didn't quite command the same degree of relaxation on the farm, it was traditional to enjoy a roast goose dinner.

It became customary, in those early years, for each house to host a Christmas party, though not quite the kind of party that would be expected today. Food seemed to be the top priority and a huge spread would be set on an elongated table in the sitting room. The table was of solid wood with carved legs and a crank handle that split open the two halves, revealing a gap to accommodate two wooden inserts. There was a distinct absence of alcoholic drinks. The only drink that vaguely resembled alcohol was homemade ginger beer, a special treat for Christmas. It was a bit like pop with a strong ginger flavour. My Mum would spend days preparing the food: a starter of boiled ham and homemade pease pudding with a tomato, lettuce and egg salad; then all kinds of homemade savoury and sweet tarts, scones, lemon meringues, egg-custards, small pastries with jelly, brandy snaps with fresh cream and custard trifles, etc. A large selection of fresh cream cakes was ordered from Bell's cake shop in Bellingham and collected on the day; but what I loved most of all were the freshly-made salmon sandwiches. I also had a craving for jam Swiss rolls and McVitie's chocolate covered wheatmeal biscuits, which I could eat for breakfast and lunch in those days. In fact, such was my liking for any kind of biscuit that my Mum had to hide them from me. After we had left the dining table, we would play various board games, whilst our parents played knock-out whist and dominoes. The whole thing would be repeated at Jack and Nancy Wood's house about a week later.

As we grew older, we advanced to darts, table tennis and snooker on a miniature table and even pop music, though, as we moved into our teenage years, we developed other interests and the parties fizzled out.

We celebrated Easter with paste eggs, an old custom, when dyed eggs were prepared and handed round to children, who rolled them on grass to see whose egg remained intact the longest. These were hens' eggs boiled in the dry outer coating of onions with flowers or herbs wrapped in old newspaper, producing unusual dyed patterns on the shell. Somehow they tasted better than a standard boiled egg.

Shrove Tuesday or Pancake Day, as we knew it, was another special day when Mum made loads of pancakes that we showered with fresh lemon juice and sugar and wrapped into a delicious roll.

West Woodburn railway station was on the single track Wansbeck line built between 1862 and 1865 with steam trains running between Redesmouth and Morpeth via Knowesgate and Scots Gap. Passenger steam trains were a regular rewarding sight and could be clearly seen from the front lawn at High Leam.

The Wannie Line, as we knew it, closed to passengers in 1952. A few goods trains continued but the last excursion train, the Wansbeck Piper, ran from Morpeth to Woodburn on 2nd October 1966. Troops destined for training at Otterburn and Redesdale Army Camps would arrive at Knowesgate or Woodburn station and complete their journey by road. By 1964, work had already begun removing the track on the

Redesmouth side of Bellingham and it was around that time I collected a trailer load of solid wooden sleepers for Bob Cragie in return for yet more home-produced honey.

Entertainment

With an abundance of firewood around High Leam, we were able to stay warm around the large open coal or log fire and hearth fender in the living kitchen and sitting room where we toasted our bread and rich smelling cheese on a toasting fork and allowed our legs to take on those unsightly circular heat blotches. With no double glazing or central heating, however, the remainder of the house remained freezing cold in winter. Frost created impressive designs to the inside of the windows as well as the outside and the only way we kept warm in bed was by using stone hot water bottles, a side effect of which was chilblains.

There was no electricity and so lighting was provided by candles and the delicate mantles of Aladdin and Tilley paraffin lamps, which were later replaced by a Calor Gas light in the kitchen and eventually generator-powered electricity. Dad had two Hurricane lamps for outdoor use. The house was frighteningly dark once you had blown out your candle and, at one stage in my young life, an owl had begun a nightly screech outside my bedroom window. I was petrified and kept my parents awake, so much so that one night, when I was creating havoc about this owl, I suddenly heard a loud bang. My Dad had decided to end the trauma and with his twelve-bore shot gun silenced the owl forever.

Mum told me that I used to sleepwalk and, one really dark night, she and Dad were awakened in their room by some very heavy deep breathing. Thinking they had an intruder, Dad apparently grabbed my leg and shouted "Gotcha!" Realising it was me, he pointed me in the direction of my room and sent me back to bed. I dread to think what a genuine burglar would have made of my Dad's attempts to make a citizen's arrest. I hated the sound of thunder and the sight of lightening scared me even more, so I always had to sit with my back to a window during thunder storms and count between the flash and the bang to give me some indication how far away it was.

Televisions had not yet arrived on the scene and evening entertainment was limited to reading the Beano or Dandy or turning on our battery-operated licensed wireless. Jigsaw puzzles were popular and I spent many hours playing with Meccano, building wheeled contraptions or things like cranes that worked with string, and Bayko building sets from which you built plastic houses. We were also shown how to make clippie mats, an old pastime of prodding strips of unwanted cloth into a patterned Hessian canvas on an adjustable wood frame, with a specially designed hand tool. These mats were used to cover the cold stone floor in the kitchen and, if you gave them a quick shake at night, you could see the minute silver fish glisten in the light.

Mum occupied many of her evenings sewing on her hand operated Singer sewing machine, darning and knitting. Wool in those days came in hanks and, before knitting, needed to be spun into wool balls, which Mum wound by hand with me holding the hank open until my arms ached. Sometimes, if I complained too much, she would loop the hank round the knobs of the huge wooden drawer set and wind the wool from there. Eventually she got one of those Knitmaster knitting machines with a rib master attachment and would knit all our jumpers for school, as well as a black and white scarf each for Brian Wood and me to support Newcastle United, who did very well in the early fifties.

With Mum and Dad being heavily committed with daily work on the farm, there was very little time for social activities other than the occasional exchange of visits with friends and relatives. The survival of the farm was paramount and everything else came second to its success. We visited my Dad's cousin Alec Taylor at Waterfalls farm above Ridsdale near Bullock's Sawmill and, in return, his wife Aunty Eva and their daughter Marion would come to High Leam where the mothers performed 'do it yourself' hair perms on each other. The liquid they used had a horrible bad egg aroma, which hung around the house for days after.

Summer holidays were nothing like they are today and amounted to a week at Whitley Bay, where Mum and Nancy Wood used to rent a house and treat Brian and me to a week at the seaside, including the Spanish City Amusement Centre and St. Mary's Lighthouse. One year, we stayed for a week in a rented caravan near Edinburgh from which we visited Edinburgh Zoo.

The nearest swimming pool to West Woodburn, I believe, was at Prudhoe and so, if there happened to be a warm sunny Sunday afternoon, Nancy Wood would take us for a stroll to The Auld Brigg at Blackburn, between East and West Woodburn, where many of the locals gathered for a picnic and a dip in the cold River Rede. We had to be on our guard against the cleggs, long-winged horse flies that hovered above the water and could give you a nasty bite.

She took us wild fruit collecting for open-tray presentations at the local Leek Show and rosehip picking on the railway banks near Hindhaugh for school collections. Mushrooms were in abundance then and we often made early morning treks around the fields to collect a helping for our breakfasts. If Dad saw any, he would bring them home in his cloth cap.

Brian's Mum and Dad took us to social events such as Harvest Festivals at the Presbyterian Church, on the corner with East Woodburn Road, and Sunday School in the Village Methodist Chapel, below White Acres Road, both having since been converted to private housing. They also took us to Whist Drives and Old Time dances in the Village Hall, in which we once danced to the famous traditional Scottish dance music accordionist, Jimmy Shand. Many of the local dances were attended by kilted Scottish Regiment soldiers visiting Otterburn Camp, some of whom would show off their ingenious sword dancing talents with energetic enthusiasm. With an old wooden HMV wind-up gramophone in the granary, Brian's Mum had taught us many of those ancient Scottish reels, polkas and waltzes, which we enjoyed putting into practice at the local hop.

For a short time, a mobile cine film business toured the local village halls, projecting black and white flickering cowboy movies on to a makeshift screen and I recall thinking how special it was when I saw my first film in Technicolor. There was also a touring fish and chip van but, living so far out of the village, we did not benefit very much. Bellingham had a more permanent cinema and Roddy Thompson's fish and chip shop, which we visited whenever we could, for one shilling and six pence - about seven and a half new pence.

I was ten and a half years old when my younger brother David was born on 28th March 1953 at Dilston Maternity Hospital, Corbridge. We knew there was something different about Mum but didn't fully understand what was going on until the last minute when I was invited to spend the night at Brian Wood's house and be informed the following morning that I had a baby brother. After being the youngest in the family for ten and a half years, I had mixed feelings of bewilderment and excitement at the same time.

In the preceding years, Dad had become a chain smoker, getting through about ten cigarettes before breakfast but now, with an extra mouth to feed, he decided to kick the habit. He replaced his Woodbines with Mint Imperials and carried some in his pocket for the rest of his life. Such was the importance of his little white Mint Imperials that I was once sent to the village to get half a pound of mints but, misunderstanding what was said and to my embarrassment, I returned with half a pound of mince instead.

PART 4   Reap what you Sow

Having the Old Fordson meant that we were now tilling the land with a Ransomes double furrow plough and disc harrows, making crop preparation and field rotation less time consuming than hitherto with horses. By treating the land with lime, slag and farmyard manure, green shoots of recovery were beginning to appear. Ploughed fields were sown with corn in the early days using a hand held wooden spreader named a fiddle because it was strapped to your shoulder, had a canvas container for the seeds and a revolving dispersal disc operated by a bow string, similar to a violin. I would see my Dad walking up and down a field with his arm going like a fiddler's elbow, though, as time moved on, they too were replaced by tractor drawn seed drills.

We did have an old horse-drawn turnip seed drill that I successfully converted to fit behind the tractor. Such mechanism meant we were producing better crops and healthier livestock, enabling an increase in the volume of cattle and sheep and consequently a better income from the various livestock markets. From filling one and a half bays in the Dutch barn in the stack yard with loose hay in the first year, we were completely filling two hay sheds, a loft over the stable, a hay hole next to the cow byres and the smaller roadside building at Woodhouse with baled hay by the time we left. This important fodder fed our outlying animals and our herds of cows, which, in the final years at High Leam, filled every stall in every byre during the winter period. We ploughed and rotated our various arable crops in the big and little back fields, the Woodhouse field, the one next to it, called the seed field, as well as the front field and the one next to it, which we called the roundabout field. None of these six fields looked as if they had been ploughed before and I don't think they have been ploughed since we left in 1965.

Six or seven dairy cows, hand milked originally, kept us all supplied with fresh milk, cream and butter. They grazed in green pasture fields throughout the milder months of the year and you could set your clock by them as they routinely gathered at the gate waiting to be brought in for milking, morning and night. They remained tied up in the cow byres during the winter months and, of course, presented their individual problems: some had warts on their teats, which, when aggravated by milking, would bleed, requiring the application of a special cream, and others had very short or small teats that could only be milked by using a finger and thumb technique.

The milk was poured into an open header tank on a hand cranked Lister separator, secured to a shelf in the pantry, an ingenious device that separated the heavier cream from the milk by channelling the liquid through a number of fast spinning dome-shaped metal cups.

After separating the cream from the milk, the residue was mixed with calf meal to feed the young calves and the remainder was mixed with swill for the pigs. The fresh cream was collected and stored in stone jars and churned to butter once a week. I never really minded separating the milk, which normally took about fifteen minutes, but churning the butter was boring and I detested it. I just hated standing in the pantry, monotonously turning the churn by hand for seemingly ages before the inspection glass cleared and the cream suddenly turned into a solid mass within the churn, a clear signal that the cream had turned to butter. Eventually, we were relieved of this burdensome task when Graham Hedley was asked to fit an electric motor to it. Mum would add some colouring to the mass and, with two wooden butter pats, make neat half pound cubes of butter, which she wrapped in greaseproof paper and sold locally.

We always kept enough milk back for the house but occasionally we ran out and it was not uncommon to serve milk straight from the cow, sometimes still warm and with the odd hayseed in the milk jug. Dad ensured that any of my cousins or friends entering the byre at milking time would certainly receive an unexpected squirt of milk direct from the cow. A twice daily helping was always given to the impatient farm cats that were afforded their freedom to control mice and any other small vermin around the buildings. The cats themselves, some domesticated, some wild, were fast breeders and, as cruel as it seemed, had to be controlled, usually by introducing a selection of new born litters to the horse troughs.

We had many free range hens, which were housed in several hen huts around the farm. Most of our eggs were packed in large egg cartons, boxed and taken away for wholesale, but Mum also sold some of the eggs locally. One of my jobs as a youngster, in addition to bringing in coal and logs, was to feed the hens and collect their eggs. They were fed and unlocked daily to scratch around the fields, then locked in at night to protect them from predators; but sometimes the cunning fox would find a way to break in and chew off their heads. We reared lots of turkeys, ordered yearly as chicks from Dickinson's near Harlow Hill, collected off the train at Redesmouth station and fattened up for the Christmas market, just as we did with Geese, Ducks, Bantams, Guinea Fowl and Cock Chickens.

Caponising cock chickens was a common form of castration, used around that time, that allowed them to put on a lot of extra weight rather than running it off by chasing after hens. The procedure was implemented on birds between six weeks and three months by injecting a hormone pellet under the skin in the nape of the neck. Apart from being a cruel operation, there was a suggestion that human female hormones were being used and, when concern was raised of a possible effect on human males through consumption, it was superseded by chemical caponisation, now itself a discontinued practice.

The poultry was starved for 24 hours prior to their fateful day in the build-up to the Festive Season, when everyone got together for poultry plucking. This took place in the building near the bottom entrance to the stack yard, where we all sat in a semi-circle around an open log fire in the corner and plucked the endless supply of dead birds handed in by my Dad. One year, I reared a pet cockerel, which I pleaded could be spared from having its neck pulled like the others. I was so pleased when Dad agreed but then got terribly upset when Brian proudly came into the plucking shed carrying a limp Rhode Island Cockerel. Apparently, he had been given permission to fell it with a shovel.

That's how life was on the farm, breeding and rearing animals without getting too attached to them or building up any feelings or compassion. At the end of the day, it was all down to plain old-fashioned business. Dad killed all the fowl by hand and I often held them whilst he did so, especially the larger species such as turkeys and geese that, after having their lives taken from them, would continue to automatically and violently flap their wings for several seconds afterwards.

The secret was to pluck them while they were still warm to avoid tearing the skin and, as time moved on, we did acquire an electric plucking machine, which I collected from a farm near Seahouses. It quickly removed the bulk of feathers, though over enthusiasm would result in skin tears and so the birds still had to be finished off by hand. We also got a winging machine which snatched out those stubborn larger wing and tail feathers. Geese were harder to pluck but a quick dip in boiling water made the process much easier. Apparently, as a young child, I had formed the opinion that it was natural for all birds to be plucked and in a moment's solitude pulled the feathers out of our pet canary.

Mum had the unenviable task of dressing the poultry, scrubbing their feet, trussing them up and generally making them presentable for market. Freezers had not quite come on to the general market and poultry would normally stay fresher for longer if left intact. By late evening, all the dressed birds were weighed, labelled and laid out in neat rows in the granary, ready to be taken for sale. Some were retained for private orders and Mum would remove their heads, wings and innards when specifically requested. The majority, however, were sold in the Christmas poultry auctions at either Crawcrook or Morpeth.

Potato picking was backbreaking work but, once again, everyone got involved and, as long as you worked uphill, it wasn't too bad. "Heed doon, arse up" my Dad used to say as our ancient tractor-drawn potato digger spun the potatoes all over the place. Once the potatoes had been stored and dried off, with a supply retained for our own domestic use, the remainder were sorted and bagged for door to door sale around the village, with the smaller ones destined for pig swill. Kale and turnips were grown for the livestock, though there was little pleasure in tediously thinning out and weeding the long rows of young turnip plants with a hoe – and no more exciting was pulling up and slicing off the tops and bottoms of the full-grown wet and often frozen swedes, prior to their storage for winter fodder. We had a hand-cranked machine, which chopped the turnips into large chips that were easier for the sheep and cattle to eat, a delicacy enjoyed by our dairy cows until we detected a turnip flavour in their milk. Subsequently, we reduced this manpower intensive work with the use of an electric fence that allowed us to hive off sections of the growing crops at a time for the livestock to self-feed.

Harvesting was by far the busiest time of the year, with healthy crops of oats being grown and, when ripe, being cut and bound into sheaves with a horse-drawn and later tractor-drawn binder. As the binder continued round the field, wild life such as rabbits and foxes were forced into the ever decreasing uncut area in the centre until finally they made a run for it. Jack Wood used to carry our twelve-bore shot gun on the tractor and take pot shots at the fleeing animals until one day, when he had left the safety catch off and to his surprise, the vibration of the tractor set off both barrels simultaneously with a deafening bang. He nearly jumped off the tractor and never carried the gun again.

A common sight in those days were acres of golden corn fields amassed with corn stooks, each made up of about eight upright sheaves, stood against each other to dispel any rain and to dry before being transferred to huge corn stacks that awaited the contractual threshing machine.

This huge four-wheeled contraption, owned by Turner Reed's of Barrasford, pulled and belt driven by a Case tractor, operated by Jack Hudson, visited the surrounding farms in turn, on a hire basis. Threshing days were communal events, with all participating farmers devoting their free time to each farm in turn on its big day and naturally expecting the same in return. This meant that there were no labour costs, though it was customary to provide food.

Mum was an excellent cook, preparing a cooked breakfast, a roast dinner, tea and supper every day of the week, though there was always a different routine on a Sunday. This was the one and only day of the week when everyone joined in with the washing up after lunch and Dad would retire for a couple of hours in bed, leaving Mum to do her weekly baking before joining him, unless, of course, we went out or received visitors. I can still see the yeast being warmed in front of the fire and smell that mouth-watering aroma lingering in the kitchen as she made bread, ham and egg pies, egg custard, rhubarb, apple and blackberry tarts, drop scones, rock buns and currant buns on a griddle. But for me nothing could beat her corned beef, potato and onion pasties.

On those threshing days, Mum and Nancy Wood served meals from huge meat roasts, prepared alongside copious amounts of boiled vegetables and baking tins filled with Yorkshire pudding, to a large number of hungry workmen in our sitting room. Then, after a pudding of apple pie and custard, it was back to work until the job was finished.

The corn was collected from the threshing machine in bags and stored loose in the granary as a food supply for poultry and animals alike; the straw was re-stacked and used as bedding for the livestock, as was the discarded chaff. To offset the cost of buying in crushed oats, we later installed our own corn crusher in the middle byre in the top courtyard. It was belt driven from a tractor pulley and, by creating an opening in the granary floor, the stored corn could be fed directly into its overhead hopper.

At the end of a hard threshing day, it was not uncommon for some farmers to afford the workforce a bit of a shindig, usually celebrated with drinks and dancing to gramophone records or a talented accordionist, whilst some indulged in a game of quoits. But the tradition phased out towards the end of the 1950s, as we witnessed the emergence of the modern combine harvester, a single-manned machine, which cut, thrashed the corn and spewed out the straw in neat rows ready to be baled, all in one operation. Of course, not all farmers could afford to buy these expensive machines but contractors were available and we hired George Richardson of The Riding, Bellingham, to harvest our corn.

Crops were improving year on year, requiring more storage for our extra volume of hay, and it wasn't long before a new hay shed was built along the back of the farm buildings to take the overflow. That was built by Robert Winston (Wince) Hardie, a professional joiner, who rode a Francis Barnett motorcycle and lived in the cottages at Sarelaw, Ridsdale, where the road turns left over The Wannies. He became a regular visitor on the farm and undertook some of the more intricate carpentry work for my parents.

Making hay was hard work then: turning the mown grass until it dried, raking it into windrows and then sweeping it into large heaps from which rounded rain-dispelling hay pikes were made. Farm implements were gradually replaced by tractor powered machinery and, with a large hay sweep attached to the front of our old Fordson, we were able to push the pikes from the back field directly to the rear of the new back hay shed. We didn't have a tractor-pulled hay bogey but, by wrapping a chain and some sacking around the bottom of the hay pikes in the other fields, we were able to drag them to the hay shed in the stack yard, often leaving behind a nest of baby field mice and a trail of rolled up hay deposits.

At about ten years of age, I had developed an insatiable interest in agricultural tractors and a newly married couple, Ian Murray and Nancy, had moved into neighbouring Cold Town farm and had become quite friendly with my Dad. Ian had just bought a brand new grey diesel Ferguson tractor with a pickup hitch and tipping trailer and I remember comparing it with our old Fordson and being so envious. I had been driving our old Fordson around the farm and working the land since I was about nine but, to my delight, Ian let me drive his 'Little Grey Fergie' from time to time and allowed us to borrow it, complete with a modern hydraulic operated pike-lifter that condemned previous methods to the history books. However, the hay still had to be forked into the hay sheds and, as it amassed beyond reach, Dad bought a huge tin-sided elevator with a temperamental water-cooled Petter engine that drove a rotating conveyor chain with tines to transfer the hay high above. Jack Murray, who lived in the cottage at Willie Bell's farm, Townfoot, East Woodburn, was a regular helper in hay time until the arrival of hay balers in the mid-1950s. His son, Graham Murray from Otterburn, later became known for his taxi and coach service, the latter earning itself a nickname 'The Passion Wagon' associated with the amorous on-board activities on its late night return journeys from surrounding village dances.

Sheep dipping was vital for the good health of sheep and, in the absence of a dipper, Dad and Jack Wood, assisted by their loyal Border Collie sheep dogs, had to herd their sheep along the road to a communal dipper on the Otterburn side of the entrance to Cold Town farm. This was time consuming and inconvenient and it was not long before they had their own dipper and sheep pens built in the second field down from the farm house.

Dad (in waterproofs and apron) dipping sheep with sons David and Andrew

The dipper was built by Riddle Brodie of Woodburn at the side of a burn where fresh flowing water was in constant supply. I spent many days as a child watching and helping my Dad submerge the sheep, one by one, into a concrete bath containing a yellow formulation of insecticide and fungicide designed to protect sheep against infestation from parasites such as ticks, lice, sheep scab, maggots, etc. Sheep dip is highly toxic and strict rules now apply to its use and disposal, which is, no doubt, why farmers now tend to use the alternative method of spraying their flocks.

I also witnessed lambs of about four months old being weaned from their mothers, having been 'lamb marked' within their first month. This was a term applied to the procedure of earmarking using a special type of pliers that takes a small piece from the end of the ear. Vaccination and medication against diseases and castration and tail docking by applying tight rubber rings that restrict blood flow were all implemented to control and improve the survival rates of lambs. The poor things didn't know whether to shake their heads, jump or kick at the painful strangulation of their testicles and tails. Now, if all that sounds cruel, it sounded quite mild when my Dad told me that they used to castrate the young lambs with their bare teeth at one time.

I learned about the categories of sheep, for example, a hogget being a one year old, a wether being a castrated male, a gimmer being a female from eighteen months until having lambs, though some farmers referred to those up to eighteen months as gimmer lambs, and cast ewes, which were those past their reproduction stage.

Sheep shearing was another big event that took Dad and Jack Wood several days. A flock, when completely dry, would be herded into the top courtyard, and then into the byre, where they were brought out individually and clipped with antiquated sheep shears, subsequently replaced with electric sheep clippers. As kids, we helped to tie up the fleeces by folding in the sides, rolling up from the tail end, and then pulling and twisting the neck area, which was wrapped round and tucked in like a belt. The fleeces were stored in the granary. On a wet day, when outside work was ruled out, they would be tightly packed into the huge Hessian sacks suspended from a beam, stitched along the top with string and finally taken away for treatment and wool marketing.

We bred young pigs and reared them in a stall in the stable until they were older and strong enough to be transferred to the open-fronted pig sties. Delivering a litter of pigs was a delicate task that usually meant staying up well into the night to monitor. A sow would produce between ten and thirteen piglets, which, driven by instinct, went in immediate search of their mother's milk, risking their short and delicate lives as their mother twisted and turned her bulky weight around them. Any neglect or failure to monitor them closely and protect them would inevitably result in some piglets being crushed or suffocated. There was invariably a runt, the smallest and weakest of the litter, which my Mum rescued to the warmth of the house and bottle fed until strong enough to join the litter. Male piglets were castrated when around three weeks old and all but two of them, one for Jack Wood and one for ourselves, subsequently went to market.

Our home-fed pigs were fattened up until the time was right for a pig killing day, a gruesome affair before the introduction of the Humane Killer, usually taking place in the colder months between October and March. Once the pig was unmercifully felled, its blood was quickly drained into a large bucket, stirred briskly and taken immediately to my Mum and Nancy Wood, who were on standby to make black pudding. Some black pudding is mixed with fat and cooked in skins but we simply mixed the blood with barley and cooked it in large oven dishes. The next task was to baste the pig skin with boiling water and, using sharp knives, scrape it all over to remove the tough bristles from its hide. It was then strung up by the back legs, the belly contents released into a large tub, later to be cleaned and used for sausage skins etc., and the carcass sawn down the middle from top to bottom. The carcass was jointed into large hams and stored in the granary where, over the next few weeks, they were treated by rubbing in saltpetre, now a controlled substance used in explosives, brown sugar and more salt until cured. The joints were wrapped in white bags like pillow cases and hung up on beams, one always being hung in the kitchen for our daily cooked breakfasts.

We turned the meat trimmings into homemade sausages and the offal into different cooking recipes; even the fat was rendered down into home cured lard. It has been said that everything except the squeal from a pig is edible. Pig killing was a brutal procedure but a necessary means to the provision of economical home-reared food produce. Any flies that had been attracted committed suicide on the sticky roll-out fly catchers that were fashionable then. They were horrible things, unhealthily blitzed by hundreds of dead flies, often seen hanging from the beams of most farm houses.

PART 5   Farm Improvements

Numerous and necessary improvements were made to the farm over the years, one of the first being the installation of a hot water system supplied from a back boiler in the kitchen fire and conversion of the bedroom adjoining the flush toilet into a bathroom by Nixon's Plumber and Electrician from Bellingham. Water supply to the farm was pumped from an in-ground Ram, a kind of self-driven pressure pump, located near a natural spring, situated about two fields down from the farm house. This supplied one header tank above the back stairs leading to the attic and another one in the garage next to the house. Over-stoking the coal fire in the colder months often resulted in the water boiling back up the pipes to the header tank, which, without warning, would erupt into a thundery bubbling geyser, spitting out over the back stairs below and solved only by rapidly draining off the excess hot water. The overflow pipe from the overhead garage tank often froze in winter, allowing excess water to cascade over our car beneath, which also froze and often resembled an igloo. The Ram was temperamental and the underground metal pipes were old and rusty but, with frequent repairs, continued for many more years, providing additionally a constant supply of water to two stone horse troughs at the far end of the front cow byres, to which any in-house animals were shepherded daily for refreshment.

Another early improvement was to concrete the area behind the farm house, past the two front cow byres and around the corner to the horse troughs and back hay shed. Dad and Jack Wood, assisted by Wince Hardie's brother Sid, completed all the work by hand: the cobble stones were lifted first, smashed into small pieces and then finally concreted over. The benefits of this were a cleaner, more presentable and manageable farm entrance and, of course, a smoother surface for our games of cricket.

Eventually, High Leam was offered for sale by the owner for about £10,000 and my Dad decided to buy it. Being now the sole owner of the farm, he was encouraged to make further modifications and, very soon, the old black-leaded fireplace was replaced with a modern fire range complete with ovens and tiled hearth. This had a much more modern appearance but it never quite lived up to its predecessor in terms of heat and efficiency. The old boiler (copper) was removed from the back kitchen and Wince boarded over the beams in the main kitchen, dispensing with the pulley-raised clothes rack and a suspended rack behind the back door where Dad used to hang his walking sticks. The old dry toilet across the back yard was modernized with a flushing unit, which, annoyingly, froze up during the winter months.

A major step forward was the installation of electricity in the farm house powered by an American Kohler petrol-driven engine and a 110 watt generator located in the riding stable adjacent to the cottage. Our generator was maintained by Edgar Thompson, a brilliant mechanic, who had a garage and repair service in Bellingham. He was tragically killed in 1955 when a car that he was working under slipped off a jack.

For the first time ever, we had lights at the flick of a switch. My parents had bought their first television for the Coronation of Queen Elizabeth II on 2nd June 1953. It was a free standing Pye television with a 12-inch screen that received its flickering black-and-white single channel signal from Pontop Pike transmitter near Consett. We often watched a blank screen with the caption 'Normal Service will be resumed as Soon as Possible' and endured interludes instead of adverts, while the terms Horizontal and Vertical Hold became new household names. It was installed by a company called Courtney's from Ponteland and I don't think their technicians will ever forget the dangerously cold and windy conditions they suffered when erecting the large vertical H-shaped aerial, later succeeded by a horizontal version, high up on the farm house chimney. Living high on the hill meant that we had a reasonable signal but experienced severe, tree-breaking gales.

Not many people had televisions and I recollect our sitting room overflowing with the locals, following an invitation being extended to anyone who wanted to watch Queen Elizabeth II being crowned in Westminster Abbey. We were all presented with Coronation Mugs at school to mark the occasion. We later repeated the invitation in May 1955 to anyone who wanted to watch Newcastle play Manchester City in the FA Cup Final at Wembley.

Life seemed to be returning to some sort of normality around that time. For the first time since the War, petrol was not rationed and rationing was lifted on sweets on 5th February 1953. I remember being given a few pennies to buy a packet of Spangles from Lizzie Wheatley's shop.

There was great excitement when we got our first Raleigh pedal cycles, complete with Sturmey-Archer three-speed gears for Christmas but, owing to the hilly terrain around us and the steep climb back to the farm, they didn't get used as much as we would have liked. The furthest we ever rode was to Elsdon to see Brian's cousin, John Anderson, and to the pictures at Bellingham. As our interest in cycling gradually waned, the bikes were duly sold.

That Kohler generator proved expensive to run and, during the same year, Dad bought a second-hand Lister diesel generator, capable of producing 240 watts, from Mick Walton at Rawfoot. It replaced the petrol model and was installed by Willie Glendinning, who extended the electricity supply to the cottage and farm buildings. The engine was designed to start up by the first switch on and shut down by the last switch off but it didn't work every time and sometimes the engine would thump away all night, much to the annoyance of Jack and Nancy Wood, who were much closer to the engine house.

The rains were often very heavy and prolonged and finally washed deep potholes and ruts in the rough stony farm road and so Dad hired Harold Rutherford to repair it. Using a lava-type waste from the disused iron works at Ridsdale, he re-laid the full length from Woodhouse but more heavy rains and running water soon penetrated the surface and, in a short time, washed most of it away. Some years later, we had the full length of the road professionally surfaced with tarmac and cattle grids installed to replace those annoying gates we had to open and shut every time we drove out.

Even a tarmac road to the farm did not convince the Local Authority that we were entitled to a weekly refuse collection, until Dad learned that other outlying farms were benefiting from the service and applied for a reduction in his rates. The new road also made it possible to include High Leam on a mobile grocery van round provided by Sid Allen's grocery shop, located at the junction of the Woodburn and Redesmouth Roads, Bellingham, and driven by Bill Dodds.

Every Thursday, the brown grocery van would arrive, enabling us to stock up on provisions for the week, and provide a rare opportunity for us youngsters to spend some pocket money on a bag of sweets or chocolate, especially chocolate covered Turkish delight.

We had started using a portable milking machine, loaned from Jim Charlton. This proved so efficient that we decided to install our own full system, which Dad acquired from the Petries of Halls Hill. The complete unit was installed by Willie Glendinning throughout the first two cow byres and powered by a petrol engine located in the cow byre in the first courtyard. Of course, it was not totally work-free in that the two milking units had to be totally stripped down and the aluminium Simplex buckets washed weekly to maintain hygiene standards. The petrol engine was later replaced by an electric motor after the farm had been supplied with full mains electricity. About the same time, we installed a supply on demand water system into the two front byers. Each cow stall was provided with a small bowl that contained a sensitive pallet in the bottom, which, when touched by the animal's nose, opened a valve and supplied water.

The supply of mains electricity inspired my Dad to build a deep litter shed with overnight light, cunningly tricking the hens into staying awake longer and naturally laying more eggs. The shed was a large ex-army sectional hut erected at the roadside in the top field by Wince Hardie. With about a hundred laying hens, it proved to be quite productive. An electric cable running from the back door of the farm house enabled the lights to be operated without venturing outside. The only downside was that the shed had no access for farm machinery and had to be tediously mucked out by hand. We had a single garage built at the side to spare our car from the annual winter ice treatment in the original garage but found that the dust from the deep litter hens was just as annoying.

PART 6   Schooldays 1953-1957

It was 1953 when, at the age of eleven and just into long trousers, I was transferred to Bellingham County Secondary School, under the Headmastership of Mr. P. G. Lucas. We were transported there and back from West Woodburn by Tait's coaches of Knowesgate, driven most of the time by Joe Ridley and occasionally by Bob Tait, who was very proud of his buses. Any misbehaviour usually resulted in the culprit being ejected from the bus and, as we were being collected one morning, someone in a pique of revenge turned off a tap marked 'fuel on / off' and, in a very short distance, the bus spluttered to a halt. Poor old Bob couldn't understand what had happened and was quite flustered as he lifted the bonnet and muttered to himself in a desperate attempt to restart the engine. Leads were removed and reconnected but, just as the situation was beginning to look serious, the fuel tap was secretly switched back on and, to the delight of Bob, the engine miraculously fired back into life.

On another occasion, the bus suffered a puncture resulting in us all having to walk the last two miles to school and, although sabotage was suspected, it was never proved. We all got up to mischief from time to time but never let it go too far and the worst offensive weapon we ever carried was a catapult. Some had air rifles but we were never allowed to have anything that resembled a real gun. Bellingham School was much bigger, with its own uniform, a navy blue jacket edged with gold braid, and taking in children from as far afield as Kirkwhelpington and the forest village of Kielder. I still remember some of the teachers: Mr. Ramsey for maths and music, Mr. Minnet for geography, Mr. Wrangham for woodwork, Jimmy O'Hanlon for science, Maggie Burns for art, and Thomas Arthur Simpson for gardening. We called him TAS from his initials and it was he who sent me to the Headmaster's office to receive six of the best for some misbehaviour in a dinnertime queue.

I was never very good at art and, when Miss Burns asked my class to draw a bonfire and Guy Fawkes, one of our friends, Brian Scott from East Woodburn, drew me a brilliant bonfire scene, which I coloured in and presented at school. Miss Burns knew instantly who had completed the drawing and severely reprimanded me for my deceit, although she did give me some credit and wrote on the bottom, 'good colouring'. Mr. O'Hanlon liked to demonstrate his favourite trick in the science room whereby, using a Bunsen burner, he heated a sealed tin can containing water, which evaporated inside the can and, as if by magic, caused the tin walls of the can to collapse as they were sucked inwards.

We went through stages when we played a lot of marbles and conkers in the autumn when they were in season. We knew where there was a horse chestnut tree near Yellow House and gathered our conkers there. Word had it that, if you slightly roasted them or steeped them in vinegar, it made them much harder and therefore difficult to defeat.

As I grew older, I enjoyed cross country running and playing in defence positions for the school football team, though I think the only team we played away was Brownrigg Camp Boarding School in Bellingham. The field formation then was a standard five man forward line, three half backs, two full backs and a goalkeeper. We had some tuition from a professional coach, who taught us the skills of ball control. I never did very well in athletics, though, which were competitively tested at the annual school sports day at

Barrasford or Humshaugh. I enjoyed woodwork, however, and made a coffee table, a table lamp stand, a stool with green and white seagrass string, a cabinet and a tea trolley.

I went on two school excursions. One was a day at a coal mine and another was a visit to the Tyneside shipyards at Wallsend and included a boat trip on the River Tyne. There was no doubt that I was more interested in the practical subjects, such as gardening, woodwork and physical exercise, than academic studies. I did, however, acknowledge my position as a senior pupil and became a prefect over my last two years at school. My heart was never really in school work, however, and I was quite pleased when the time came to leave, as I had become more interested in work back on the farm.

It was around 1956 when the telephone was installed at High Leam via an underground cable mole-ploughed in from Woodhouse across the fields. The handset was located in the passage near the front door with an extension bell over the door of the kitchen. The phone became an instant success as it brought us all into contact with the outside world. I still remember the telephone number 236 to this day, though some extra digits have since been added. Dad would disappear about twice a week and have a 'craic' with his new acquaintance, John Raine, who farmed Low Park at East Woodburn.

There was no direct dialling then and to make a connection it was necessary to dial '0' for the operator, quote the calling and the desired contact numbers and wait to be put through. Prior to that we used the old red telephone kiosk in the village at the end of the Yellow House Road, opposite Jim Charlton's butcher shop, where the same procedure applied, but first it was necessary to insert four old pennies and, upon hearing your contact at the other end, press button 'A'. If there was no reply, you just pressed button 'B' and got your money back.

Our local friends from the village liked to visit High Leam. One of them was John Wright, who often went fox hunting. He went on to be Licensee at the Redesdale Arms on the A68 near Rochester, known as the First and Last because it is still the first Pub coming into England and the last going out. John and his wife Hilda later became proprietors of The Bay Horse, an eighteenth century coaching inn beside the River Rede at West Woodburn.

The fox hounds of the Border Hunt were kennelled at Overacres Farm, where any dead cows were donated by local farmers to feed the dogs. They were a regular sight around the fells of Woodburn, responding to the melodious tones of a hunting horn carried by John Dixon of Rochester, the Whipper-in. The annual Hunt Ball at Bellingham was a huge social event and was often serenaded by that hunting horn as the night wore on. John's brother, Peter, lived at The Stobbs and made show-standard walking sticks.

We all had our ponies and one named Justice had been wintered in the stable and treated with crushed oats, making it a risky mount, but, apparently, I insisted on going for a ride. Against Dad's better judgment, he let me go, only for me to be thrown and dragged through ditches and mud by one of the stirrups. Luckily, I escaped without serious injury but you could say that Justice got me in the end.

We had begun to show black-faced sheep in agricultural shows at Bellingham, Rochester, Falstone, the County Show at Corbridge and as far away as Gilsland, Haltwhistle and Allendale. At the Royal Show at Newcastle in 1956, I recall meeting up with Jonty Hutchinson from Lee Hall, who was quite a young teenager and made front page news in the Newcastle Journal for winning the tractor driving competition. Jack Wood and John Raine really knew their sheep. They selected their own very best animals, washed and groomed them and caringly prepared them for show.

Brian and I often travelled to the shows with the sheep in the back of the wagon just to get into the show ground free. Then we helped out by holding the sheep whilst a judge expertly studied their finest qualities and awarded first, second and third prizes. We regularly got selected in the first three places, occasionally winning a show championship and the odd silver cup. Dad said that the prize money never justified the effort and that it was more of a way for people getting to know you and your livestock.

Bellingham Show: Jack Wood and his undefeated Black-faced ewe lamb

Well-bred, black-faced sheep were a sought-after breed and prize tups were expensive, often hired out to other farmers to service their flocks and attracting thousands of pounds at auction. Our prize tup 'Sam' was the business and did his best to produce new generations of quality black-faced lambs. I can still remember where we eventually laid him to rest and Brian has reminded me that we even placed a homemade wooden cross on his grave.

The hoppings (fairground attractions) always arrived in Bellingham to coincide with the Bellingham Show and established themselves on the Fairstead alongside the Hareshaw Road, on the other side of the railway line from the former Bellingham Mart ground. The hoppings, a fraction of the size of Newcastle Town Moor, was a North Eastern name for a fairground, derived from dancing or hopping in bygone days; they were still extremely popular at that time and enjoyed by all. Even the Black-Faced Sheep Breeders' annual ball at Bellingham was known locally as the Tup Hop.

A few local farmers, George Elliott from the Cragg, John Scott of the Brigg, John Raine, Jack Wood and ourselves formed a committee and organised our own sheep show in the field behind the West Woodburn Institute Hall, coinciding with the Village Leek Show. We borrowed the sheep pen fence hurdles from Bellingham Show Committee, providing that we collected and restored them under the grandstand on their show ground. Woodburn Show flourished for several years before being wound up in the mid-Sixties, with farmers bringing prize sheep from far and wide. Other attractions included small craft and side stalls, a coconut shy, Cumberland and Westmorland Wrestling and hound trailing where an aniseed trail was laid for trained sniffer dogs to follow, with bookies taking bets on the winners.

Although Andrew and I had been driving around the farm from an early age, it was lawful to drive tractors on the roads from the age of sixteen and by the time that Andrew was seventeen and learning to drive cars, we had an Austin of England pickup with a wooden windowed canopy fitted with folding wooden seats on the back. It was ideal for carrying sheep but you were isolated and often cold if you were a rear passenger and it wasn't long before Dad sold that and bought a brand new Hillman Minx Estate VVK 308 from George and Jobling of Hexham. It had a column gear change and, with double doors at the back, was ideal for carrying sheep in a special carrying crate made to fit by Wince Hardie. This was the last car we had that started with the separate self-starter button, subsequent models moving on to the modern technique of starting from a simple turn of the ignition key. It was also normal for previous cars to have the headlamp dip switch on the floor next to the clutch and a manually operated choke control.

Having experimented with different breeds of dairy cattle, Ayshires, Shorthorns, Jerseys and Guernseys, Dad finally settled on a herd of Friesians, selling them as first calving heifers at Hexham Mart on a market day. They were hugely popular as dairy cows and often won prizes as best in their class. Cows were generally able to calve themselves but, as always, there were occasions when they needed a little help. This usually involved putting some baler twine around the front feet of the calf and pulling it free. It was not always that straightforward, however, and there were many occasions when calves were badly positioned for birth or even dead or a cow would push out her back body and we had to call out a costly vet from Hexham, a condition of which was that you provided a bucket of warm soapy water and a towel – not surprising when you saw where he buried his upper limb to his armpit. Of course, our heifers were intended as dairy cows, which meant that their calves were taken from them the minute they hit the ground and reared by hand. Getting them to drink from a bucket was helped by putting your hand in the bucket and allowing them to suck your finger.

We progressed to having our cows artificially inseminated, a task previously undertaken by the resident farm bull that was almost impossible to contain within the dry-stone walls, fences and gate confines of a field whenever he detected the call of a heifer coming into season. The young, first-calving heifers did not like being milked and some would kick out at anyone who dared to venture near, let alone succumb to a milking machine. Dad, who would carefully seat himself on his three-legged milking stool with his head pressed against the cow, preferred to use his own traditional methods, like tying one leg back or tying a rope tightly around the animal's waist or getting someone like me to push their tail upwards and forwards, making it extremely awkward for them to kick. Anyone holding the tail and facing such an unsightly scene just prayed the cow's grass diet had not been too rich!

Most calves were reared on the farm, although a few were sold to local breeders, such as the Robsons of Chesterhope, usually seeking a replacement after a sudden loss. Bull calves were castrated with metal clams, a big pair of double action pincers that painfully nipped and permanently damaged the testicle cords. I saved a white Shorthorn bull calf from that agonising fate and reared him in the tin shed situated in the front field but, as he grew older and bigger, he became quite frisky and dangerous. He began by nudging me with his nose, whenever I went to feed him, but then started to lift me off the ground; so Dad decided it was time for him to move on. As young bulls have a reputation for being unpredictable, we decided that he would attract a better price, if he were seen being controlled and led around the ring by someone as young as me. As I paraded him before the auctioneer and an array of potential buying farmers at Bellingham Mart, he followed me faultlessly and sold at a fair price, although we perhaps expected him to make more.

Tuesday was market day at Hexham and Dad never missed a day at the mart. With shoes polished, best stick in hand and a pocket full of crumpled one and five pound notes as 'luck money', he would set off at about nine o'clock, leaving Andrew and me to load our latest prize heifer into the cattle wagon. One Tuesday morning, we had inadvertently left the farm gate open and the newly-calved heifer escaped. By the time we rounded her up, she was dirty, dishevelled and had run off most of the volume of her udder. Communication was nothing like it is now and Dad just had to find out the hard way as we loaded her on to the wagon and sent her off to the mart. He couldn't believe his eyes when he saw her coming off the wagon at Hexham and, to say the least, he was displeased and didn't win any prizes that day. On the rare occasion when something went wrong, we could always contact the mart office and get a message to Dad for his advice or to collect a vital part that had suddenly failed on our machinery – but we chose not to get in touch that morning.

Occasionally, I would accompany Dad to the mart and, although I enjoyed listening to the latest farming gossip around the byres and auction ring, there was clearly a lack of enthusiasm on my part in dealing with livestock. Eventually, when I got tired of the monotonous drone of the auctioneer, I would wander off around the various agricultural supply stores such as Rickerby's and Fewsters to check out the latest farming machinery. Mum and Nancy Wood often took the opportunity to go with Dad for a day out, browsing around the shops and the busy fresh produce market in the ancient Shambles and having lunch at 'Nichols' Café.

One frosty Tuesday morning, they were all on their way to Hexham in our Hillman Minx and had only got to the village when the windscreen froze over and caused them to crash into the back of a stationary Elsdon Coal wagon. The car was badly damaged and the Police were called. Dad pleaded not guilty to the accident, saying he was operating the heater controls at the time. He thought that was a plausible defence but was convicted of driving without due care and attention.

For animal haulage, we used two Otterburn firms, sometimes Joseph Foster & Son, with driver Tom MacDonald, but usually John W. Reed, who used distinctive sounding two-stroke Commer lorries in the 1950s and 1960s. Our regular driver was John Thomas (Tot) Dickson, who was well known in the farming community, and Alwyn (Olly) Tully became another regular driver. The business survived the death of John W. Reed in 1956 and continued to be run by the family, notably Michael Reed, for over thirty years.

Farm machinery had continued to improve throughout my secondary school years, with modern combine harvesters replacing threshing machines and bales of hay taking the place of hay pikes. It was 1953 when my Dad had arranged for some hay to be baled by a contractor, who stipulated that there must be at least two fields to make it worthwhile. Two fields of fresh long grass were duly mown but the contractor failed to appear, exposing a large crop of hay to bad weather and ruin. My Dad vowed that would never happen again and, the following year, he bought a new McCormick International Harvester B45 Mk I baler from Rickerby's at Hexham.

Dad decided to take up local contract hay baling, charging six old pence a bale, with an extra penny added for Jack Wood, who became a familiar sight during the summer months travelling on our old Case tractor to The Steel, The Cragg, The Hole, Briaredge, The Newton, Woodburn Hill, Yellow House, Low Park, Hole Mill, Halls Hill and many other farms. Andrew left school in 1955 and started work for my Dad, who set him up in contract work the following summer with a McCormick International Harvester B45 Mk II baler and replaced the faithful old Fordson with a second-hand diesel Fordson Major tractor, bought from Patterson's at Hexham.

The Mk II baler was similar to the Mk I except that it was slightly faster and the outside string box had been moved to the inside, making it narrower and easier to get through farm gates. Whenever we secured a deal with a salesman, he would reward us with a penknife or similar handy work tool. I collected penknives and still have a few, some of which have been used and others are still new in their boxes.

We began to wonder if we had made the right decision in buying the Fordson Major, as, when the delivery low loader got stuck off the road and couldn't be moved by this shiny blue tractor, it was necessary to unload the departing old Fordson, which effortlessly towed the wagon to hard ground. The next time we tried to start its replacement, the solenoid switch burnt out and our excitement began to wane as we had to wait for a repair under the guarantee. That apart, the new Fordson Major did turn out to be a vast improvement over the old Fordson. In 1956, we bought our first petrol paraffin Ferguson tractor from Crag House at Falstone and, in a short time, equipped it with a hydraulic drill-plough, a cultivator and a twin-furrow plough that earned the old Ransomes trailer-plough a place on the scrap heap.

Health and Safety rules were less stringent in those days, with few, if any, safety guards around power-driven machinery. Many farm machine operators suffered, at the very least, serious injury from an unguarded power drive shaft at the rear of a tractor, which was notorious for snatching any loose clothing, with no means of escape and probable fatal consequences. The longer you worked with power-driven machinery, the more confidence you gained and the more complacent you became in maintaining and cleaning those awkward areas during operation. Any carelessness or lack of respect could easily result in a limb being trapped or amputated in the moving parts.

Some years later, the Case tractor suffered some serious engine damage and, following its replacement by a 'live drive' Fordson Major, MNL 324, was broken up by a scrap metal dealer near Woodburn disused railway station. 'Live drive' was a clever 2 part clutch system, which, by pressing the clutch pedal halfway down, allowed you to momentarily bring the tractor to a standstill whilst the power-driven machine continued operating. This was ideal for baling heavy crops and allowed the machine's workload to catch up with the pace of the tractor periodically rather than allowing it to overload and 'choke'. Stopping the power-driven machine was achieved by depressing the pedal fully home.

We had installed a 500-gallon diesel tank near the gate into the farm yard and it seemed right that we traded the petrol paraffin Ferguson in for a diesel model, bought from Fewsters of Hexham. Diesel engines provided more power and, being on a hill farm, we had larger 12-inch tyres fitted for extra grip. We also replaced the original B45 Mk I baler with another B45 Mk II, though these balers were comparatively slow by today's standards and prone to breakdown and loss of precious time awaiting the attendance of fitters from Hexham. However, they were protected by a sheer bolt safety device that secured two flywheels together and, if put under undue pressure, would snap. The sheer bolts were easily replaced and we always had a constant supply with us. At the time of replacing the old B45, none of us had been aware that a new, faster and more reliable B46 Baler was about to hit the market and Dad was resentful that the suppliers had failed to mention this fact.

With extreme difficulty in meeting excessive demands on the few good haymaking days that came along, Raymond Marshall became our regular fitter and breakdown saviour, who later progressed to selling John Deere tractors. If we were really struggling, Billy Dobson would lend his tractor and baler to help us through the busy time, though we eventually got Raymond Marshall to rig our Ferguson up for the baler that I used regularly for the Patterson's of Broomhope. Andrew baled a lot of hay for the Rogerson's at Cottonshope near Catcleugh, where, one day, when he was going uphill, the thrust from the baler ram sprung the towing hitch pin, leaving Andrew looking on helplessly as the baler sped off backwards towards the A68 England to Scotland trunk road and Catcleugh Reservoir. Thankfully, however, it veered sideways and flipped over before it reached the road.

Making silage was not so popular in the 1950s and farmers tried to forecast good weather before mowing a field of rich green grass to make good hay, otherwise several days of rain would turn the mown grass brown and destroy its appeal to winter livestock. St. Swithin's Day (15th July) was always anticipated with close attention, for tradition has it that the weather on St. Swithin's Day will continue for forty days. In one long, wet summer, the hay was so bad that we had to purchase drums of commercial treacle to encourage the livestock to eat it. Jack Wood often said that good hay required the sun baled into it and, on the rare sunny days we had, the bales were light, smelt fresh and made good winter fodder. It's not hard to imagine why, as hay baling contractors, we were everyone's friend on good haymaking days but not so popular whenever we let someone down for whatever reason, particularly if the weather turned to rain. During those haymaking months, it was daily routine to check the weather forecast and optimistically tap the weather barometer, eagerly willing it to move in the right direction.

Wet summers made haymaking difficult, as farmers struggled to get the hay dry for baling; any dampness in the hay would heat in a hay stack or hay shed and, in extreme cases, could create a spontaneous combustion. Dampness also made the bales heavier, which, in my time as a farm worker, were manhandled much more than today and anyone who worked with hay bales will tell you that a few hours picking them up by their binding baler twine left your hands blistered and raw. Hay bales also absorbed rain and needed to be retrieved as soon as possible to get shelter from the weather elements, otherwise it was necessary to stook them on their ends, usually in fours, with the string knots at the bottom, to help dispel rainwater. With the help of local casual workers, we mostly led our bales home in an evening. By deploying two or three men in the field, we were well organised, with Andrew and me on two tractors and trailers, alternately transporting and reversing never ending loads of bales into the hay sheds, where they were carried aloft by a modern Lister bale elevator and stacked for winter fodder.

Reversing trailers can be a difficult skill to learn but one that most farm workers develop through everyday work on the farm. I recall that I once put mine to the test by reversing a trailer for the whole distance from Woodhouse to High Leam, approximately one mile, just for the fun of it.

The Lister elevator was also useful for transferring our sacks of animal foods, such as pig and calf meal, cow cake, beet pulp, etc., through the rear upper double doors of the granary, whenever we received our monthly supplies, ordered through our visiting salesman, Bill Lawrence, and delivered by Tom Foster on behalf of the Northern Farmers' Trading Association at Bellingham. The hundredweight sacks were previously carried up the steep granary steps manually by Dad and Jack Wood, who both maintained that they were more manageable than some two hundredweight sacks that were in circulation at one time. The granary was divided into two parts at slightly different floor levels and we constructed our own ramp so that deliveries could be transferred from one end to the other by sack barrow.

In addition to the casual hay time labourers being paid an hourly rate, Mum always made supper for them and, during the winter, we delivered them a free trailer-load of fresh farmyard manure for their gardens. This manure emanated from our daily routine, mucking out all the farm byres that housed our cattle over the winter months and was often mixed with dry straw, baler twine and afterbirths from cow calving. Our mucking out procedures took up most of the morning and resulted in a full muck spreader load that we routinely emptied in the pasture fields. The cattle quickly adjusted to this daily routine, even remembering and navigating their way back to their own individual stalls after being herded to the horse troughs for water refreshment. As spring approached, the cattle were happy to join the fresh green pastures and the old muck spreader was taken to the river at The Auld Brigg for its yearly wash and removal of the baler twine that had wrapped around its revolving spindles.

Great interest was always shown in our garden, a vast area with rich soil and numerous established gooseberry, red currant and blackberry bushes, rasp canes, strawberry plants and rhubarb roots, the produce of which went into homemade jam, tarts and puddings. Part of the garden was enclosed by a ten-foot high stone wall and was hived off for Jack Wood. On our side, we grew potatoes, carrots, parsnips, radishes, beetroot, lettuce, cabbage, peas, beans, shallots, onions and leeks, using jam jars with the bases tapped out to protect the small plants and encourage growth. The onions and leeks were planted in the same fertile beds every year and carefully nurtured to a high standard for the local Leek Show.

Living on a farm meant that we had lots of manure for the garden but for the leeks we mixed raw droppings from the sheep pens with water in a forty-gallon oil drum to produce the most vile substance I have ever had the misfortune to smell and with tubes directed to the roots of special plants. We fed them regularly with this green liquid, producing such amazing results that I think they would have thrived on the smell alone. The secret was not to overfeed them and exceed the maximum measurements required by the Show Judges. We were in competition with some very experienced leek growers in the village and, whilst we often came in the top three, the first prize invariably went to someone else.

PART 7:   Life after School 1957+

I left school at the age of fifteen in late 1957 and immediately started working for my Dad, building on the experiences I had already learnt around the farm, particularly with regard to the various types of livestock, delivering calves and lambs, milking cows, rearing poultry and sheep shearing. Now that's a job I found totally monotonous, spending a full day clipping sheep after sheep after sheep. We were still using the old sharp-pointed hand clippers and, as you tipped your sheep into position and opened up the fleece down one side, clipping beneath the old wool, it was difficult not to leave the occasional nick in the skin.

The wet hill land was a detrimental factor in the wellbeing of our sheep: they demanded so much attention and almost became walking pin-cushions with the various inoculations needed to combat diseases and infections. We provided them with blocks of salt lick, which contained the necessary minerals so that they could adjust their intake according to their needs. Many developed foot rot, which we tried to pre-empt by running them through a chemical foot trough but, in extreme cases, we had to pare their hoofs with a sharp knife, occasionally damaging a blood vessel that we stemmed by applying a handful of cobwebs and a special foot rot paste or spray. With about 400 sheep to look after, Jack Wood took care of the lambing, often in the most atrocious April weather conditions. With limited indoor space available for lambing pens, only the weakest earned a place of shelter, the remainder having to take their chance with the cold and the rain, often with dire consequences.

Dehorning cattle was quite a common procedure on farms around that time to minimise the risk of injury to humans and other animals, though today most cattle have their horns disbudded by chemical cauterisation before they reach two months of age. Getting a full-grown cow to stand still whilst you sawed off its horns was no easy task and for this purpose we had a cattle crush with a head gate and neck trap lever. This was a heavy, portable metal-framed type of cage that held and restrained a single animal at a time, yet provided a safe area for operators attending to the nervous animal from the outside. The Protection of Animals (Anaesthetics) Act 1954 as amended made it an offence for cattle to be dehorned without the use of anaesthetic and, once this had been administered, the horns were sawn off with an embryotomy wire that with friction became hot and cauterised any affected blood vessels.

Herding livestock was totally dependent on our ever faithful, intelligent and active Border Collie dogs that had a natural herding drive but also sensitivity to human voice and touch that required careful handling and training. Two such dogs are still in my thoughts. One was named Cap because of the white patch on his head. He suffered some poor health, in particular, a bad case of mange, but my Mum nursed him to a full recovery. The other was called Moss, a brilliant sheep dog that, despite suffering a broken front leg, lived to a ripe old age. Jack Wood lost a brilliant young Collie bitch, which he kept tied up to prevent it chewing its way under doors. The poor thing had wrapped its lead around a pole, thus using up too much slack before jumping over a partition and hanging herself. Good sheep dogs were not always available and those that were well trained could be quite expensive. William Leslie (Les) Dixon of Carlcroft in Upper Coquetdale was a good breeder and we got some of ours from there.

PART 8   Redesdale Work & Play

Being a hill farm, High Leam was not productive enough to pay four wages and so I was encouraged to take outside employment and help out at home in the busy summer months. So, for the first time, I ventured into the outside world or, at least, the length and breadth of Redesdale.

Postman: My first job was a relief postman, helping Doug Scott with his extra workload over the Christmas period. He had a little post van that he kept in one of those buildings near to Lizzie Wheatley's shop and delivered mail locally, including the outlying farms. It made me realise just how patient he must have been on his own, opening and shutting all those farm gates, six days a week. Dad wanted me to serve my apprenticeship as an agricultural engineer but this would have meant leaving home and, on the wages offered, life would have been fairly limited.

Draining: Jim Charlton at Tenter House had started land draining and was looking for someone to work with his brother-in-law Harry Tittcomb and Cecil Wood of East Woodburn on his sheep-draining outfit on the fells above the river Coquet at Barrowburn. I accepted the job but didn't know what to expect as we set off early one Monday morning in Cecil's old Austin car and arrived at Barrowburn, still in darkness. From there, we set off walking from the back of the farm up a steep hill side and eventually came across a huge single-furrow land drainage plough, which was attached to an International Harvester BTD-6 Crawler Tractor.

It was my job to walk behind this monster as it ploughed deep, open sheep-drains across the open fells and pull out with a three-pronged 'hack' any lumps of earth that had fallen in behind, as well as tidy up any drain junctions with a draining spade. Cecil and Harry were great guys to work with but they never stopped and I learned that, if we clocked up a certain number of chains (a chain being 22 yards) in a week, we earned a bonus. The bonus threshold must have been carefully calculated as we only achieved it once in the time I worked there. My wage then was about seven pounds per week and I felt quite well off until my Dad suggested I give Mum some of it for my board. I was a bit surprised by this but I was young, working hard and did eat healthily and so it was only fair to pay something towards my board and lodgings.

Mum made me the best ham and tomato sandwiches but my mistake was telling her with the result that I got them every day in my bait box until I was fed up with them.

We spent long hours of unrelenting, strenuous work but it was a super outdoor job in the fresh air, walking for miles on the most scenic open fell ground. There was no shelter on those bleak hills and, being so exposed to the elements, we experienced some of the most appalling driving rain, sleet, snow and severe frost conditions. But this never stopped us. We kept dry with waxed coats, over-trousers and heavy duty waterproof mitts with woollen gloves inside and the very nature of the job kept us warm anyway. While we were working at Troughend, we were asked to transport a dead sheep in our work van to the vet at Hexham in order to establish its suspicious cause of death. It must have been dead for a few days as it stank sickeningly rotten and, although we nearly froze to death with all windows wide open, the smell became so unbearable that we bought a bottle of Dettol, which, when mixed with the putrid stench of the rotting animal, seemed worse than ever and lingered in the van, in our nostrils and on our clothes for days after.

Some of the peat bogs we drained were so soft that even the crawler tractor was getting stuck and so we had extra plates welded on to the tracks to make them about nine inches wider and give additional traction. The peat bogs stank rotten and often contained nests of black water rats which, after being disturbed, could be seen swimming along behind the plough as it drained the water from the soggy, smelly mass.

It was inevitable sometimes that a rat would become impaled on a tine of the hack and you would hear its teeth grind on the metal in a final death throe. We had a winch fitted on the back of the crawler tractor for pulling the plough through such bogs, which meant that the diesel tank had to be relocated on the side next to the driver seat.

I used to carry three flasks of tea and three bait boxes to help offset my insatiable appetite and, as usual, we hung our bait bags on the headlamps of the tractor: the golden rule was never to separate yourself from your bait. One morning, after we had stopped for breakfast, we realised that the bait bags had not been hung in their usual place and soon found three flat packs squashed into the mud where the crawler tractor had just been. Tragically, Harry Tittcomb died suddenly on 4th May 1961, aged just 42.

Back to the Farm: As the hay season approached, I returned to work on the farm and, although I was not yet old enough to drive on the roads, I was sent out with the little grey Fergie and a tractor-converted trailing Bamford reaper on metal wheels to mow hay for Bob Rickelton at Hole Mill. I loved working in hay time with that fresh smell of newly-mown grass drying under the sun. I just enjoyed working with tractors and farm machinery, messing about with spanners and getting my hands greasy.

Bob Rickelton had no farm machinery and we made hay for him for years. If there was a choice between working with sheep and driving a tractor, I went for the tractor every time. Dad said that I was tractor daft. Rather than take a chance with the law by going the road way through the village, I risked the short distance along the main road from Woodhouse to the track on the right down to The Auld Brigg and back on to the quiet main road on Darney Bank above East Woodburn. In time, we replaced the Bamford reaper with a much faster power-driven, rear-mounted, hydraulically lifted and lowered, five-foot finger cutter bar, capable of cutting anything as long as the knives were kept sharp.

For those unfamiliar with farm machinery, a cutter bar attaches and forms a part of the tractor, cutting a five-foot swathe of grass alongside it just above ground level. Any unsuspecting animals hiding in the long grass might see the tractor approaching but would not see the extended cutter bar heading straight for them under the grass, which is exactly what happened to one of our farm cats, which leapt off frantically across the field obviously in great pain. In that very same field, a rabbit suffered a similar fate but lost all four legs and had to be instantly relieved of its agony. Surprisingly, some months later, our missing, presumed dead, farm cat returned home, desperately lean and walking on three legs, though happily went on to live a long and healthy life.

I sharpened the knives myself with a reaper file and learned that filing downwards on the numerous triangular sections created a fine unwanted under-lip, whereas upward strokes didn't and made them much sharper. Being mounted on the back of the tractor enabled us to travel faster and further afield to Fourlaws, Halls Hill and other surrounding farms. We turned hay at Hole Mill and double-rowed it into windrows for baling with a Vicon Lely hay turner, an earlier wheeled version of the hydraulic-mounted acrobat that turned the hay with two sets of three spindly fans driven by ground friction as you towed it along. By relocating all six fans in a line, we were able to rake two hay swathes into one, ready for baling. Raising and lowering the turner fans from the ground was tediously achieved by dismounting the tractor and cranking two handles at the rear. Soon, however, we had an accessory fitted so that it could be quickly operated by pulling a rope from the tractor seat.

The Vicon Lely was a competitor for the more squat, blue Bamford turner, though ours would slip about on hillsides, particularly in wet summers, and, instead of turning the hay, the friction-driven fans had a tendency to push the turner sideways down the hill. The problem was solved by attaching an anti-slip disc that cut into the ground and stabilised the machine as it rotated alongside the back wheel. We also had a wuffler, a small hay tedder, which was power-driven from the tractor and made an excellent job of shaking up the hay but it was only wide enough for one hay swathe. As most modern machines accommodated two, it took double the normal time to complete a whole field.

Whatever machinery we had at our disposal was committed to contract work, far or near, and I spent one whole day travelling to Byrness and back to shake up a field of hay with the wuffler. As tractors in those days had a maximum speed of about eighteen to twenty miles per hour, about three hours were spent travelling.

We had purchased a new turnip seed drill, which, depending on which seed belt we fitted, would deposit single turnip seeds at a given distance, thus removing the burdensome need to hoe and single out the delicate young plants. It was hugely successful, unless a seed got wedged in a hole in the belt, causing unwanted gaps between the plants, which of course, did not become apparent until they germinated.

Young Farmers' Club: With the darker nights approaching, Andrew and I found ourselves at a loose end in the evenings and so we joined the Young Farmers' Club at Bellingham, run by Bryce Rennison, now at Hole Mill, and two of the Bell brothers from Woodpark, Wark. We met once a week in a room at Bellingham School, where we listened to guest speakers and organised events like ploughing matches and inter-club quiz competitions.

I remember Bryce preparing us with the answers to anticipated questions, such as what is the percentage of butterfat in milk (about 3.25%) and who is the Minister for Agriculture, etc., with the result that we always did quite well in the competitions, whether at home or away. Some spare places were obtained to attend a residential weekend at the Northumberland College of Agriculture, Kirkley Hall. I volunteered, as did Brian Anderson, formerly of Cleughbrae, attending lectures and demonstrations and generally having a good time, though things did get a bit rowdy in the dormitory on the last night.

On the day before we attended, I had cut my right thumb badly on a rusty tin sheet and was prescribed penicillin capsules to combat infection. I had never taken dissolving capsules before and, not being aware that they had to be taken whole, I opened the capsules and swallowed the powdery contents, with such devastating gastronomic results that I wouldn't recommend to my worst enemy, especially being away from the comforts of home for a few days.

I learned a great amount from the Young Farmers' Club about debating and guest speaking and made my first attempt at speaking in public after William (Bill) Robson of Chesterhope had given a talk to Woodburn Youth Club about his Monte Carlo Rally driving experiences. When he had finished, there was an uneasy silent pause, so I took the opportunity, stood up, thanked him on behalf of the club and suggested that we show our appreciation in the usual way, which went down very well.

Village Dances: The beginning of 1960s saw Rock 'n Roll catch on and, once Andrew had passed his driving test, we borrowed Dad's car to travel to the numerous Friday night village dances that were taking place all around us. A group called The Rebels was very popular and, after meeting at the Fox and Hounds, we travelled to wherever they were playing. This lively group was one of many that played the latest hits on a rotational basis every Friday night in village halls at Rothbury, Thropton, Whittingham, Otterburn, Rochester, Elsdon, Byrness, Falstone, Wark, Bellingham, Capheaton, Cambo, Middleton and, of course, West Woodburn.

It was not unusual for us to visit two or three separate dance halls in one night. Andrew, myself and two others decided one Friday night to drive down to Kielder for a few pints at the Castle before returning to the dance at Falstone. As the pubs, however, stopped serving at 10.30 pm with 20 minutes drinking up time and we were late getting there anyway, we ordered a round of drinks each, sixteen pints in all. We were quite pleased with ourselves for getting two gallons of beer on the table before closing time until someone casually mentioned that there was an extension until 11.30 pm.

Saturday nights were reserved for the weekly dance at Bellingham, although the dances at Otterburn Club and Otterburn Army Camp were very popular while they lasted. At the age of sixteen or seventeen, and now having a smooth tarmac road up to the farm, I bought a second-hand racing cycle with derailleur gears so that I could meet up with friends at Bellingham on a Saturday evening. Fortunately, I was able to cheat on the return journeys by hitching a lift home (bike included) with Andrew in Dad's car after the Dance.

We just walked sometimes to events in the village but the absence of any street lighting made walking home alone through three pasture fields on a dark, moonless night an unnerving experience. Sometimes, you could not see a hand in front of you and tripping over a sleeping sheep or a cow was heart-pounding stuff. But when one of the farm ponies sneaked up behind you and gave you a sudden nudge in the back, it was enough to make you high jump for England.

Draining: In that very same autumn, I returned to my job in open land drainage, from which I was transferred to a gang wiring field drains, working alongside Harold Bullock, Ted Elliott from Little Ridsdale and another young man, Robert 'Sporty' Bell. We occasionally met at the farm buildings on the road to Bellingham and, one morning, we had been delayed until nine o'clock when Jim Charlton arrived. He was furious that we were still there and I will never forget his quickly calculated outburst: "Four men here for two hours, that's a day's work for one man".

Field drains usually comprise 3"x12" porous red clay, kiln-hardened pipes, laid in a line about twenty yards apart and three feet beneath the surface; but they may become furred up or blocked, causing boggy areas above ground. Some had been sabotaged, believed by prisoners of war, who were enlisted to lay drains during World War Two and, if not correctly supervised, would deliberately lay a pipe transversely. Our job was to pull a one chain length of special wire, with a rag attached, through the drains. To do this, we dug holes, maybe six or eight a day, at distances of about twenty yards along the drain to access the pipes. We had various means of finding the drains. One involved a long bradawl, which showed red stains on the tip, if you were lucky enough to strike a pipe. Another was to dig beneath the turf and look for signs of soil mixed with clay, an indication that the earth had been excavated at some point – but our main success was down to the expertise of our foreman. Pushing the wire through the drain in the first place often met with obstructions but, by turning it with a starting-handle shaped end, it was usually possible to get through. If not, you just had to dig another hole. It wasn't a very satisfying job, particularly under inclement weather conditions, when, for most of the time, I was working with my hands in cold or freezing muddy drain water, causing painful keens, or split finger ends.

Tractor Driving: I had heard that a vacancy had arisen for a tractor driver in the firm, with a gang laying new field drains. I asked Jim Charlton for the job and, without any hesitation, he set me on. It was a fine Monday morning when I met Howard Maughan, Jim Charlton's fitter and mechanic, at Yellow House Farm, as arranged. He introduced me to a machine that only I would operate for the foreseeable future: a Fordson Power Major tractor with wide, water-filled rear tyres for traction, a hydraulically-operated bulldozer blade on the front and a thirty-foot long trailer on the back. He then directed me to Gorfenletch Farm near Longhorsley. Howard was a real character, whom I got to know well over the following years. He lived at White Acres, where we were always welcome for a first-foot drink at New Year. Having not yet passed my driving test and with 'L' plates attached, I arrived on a vast land-drainage site and was greeted by the foreman Bill Richardson, a land drainage legend, who explained my new job to me in five minutes flat. A huge Priestman excavator on tracks was ripping out open trenches in which three-inch diameter drain pipes were being expertly laid in line by Bill and protectively covered with a layer of soil by a helper.

My Dad and Andrew taught me to drive and, having been driving around the farm from an early age and already driving tractors on the road for Jim Charlton, I was a little over-confident in my driving ability and applied for a test straightaway. But I had a quick reality check when I failed. The examiner asked me to use hand signals only, which I thought was a bit unfair. I re-applied immediately and, with renewed vigour and concentration, qualified as a full driving licence holder in early 1960.

My job was to lead out and stack the pipes in piles of fifteen every five yards and back fill the newly laid drains with the tractor blade. The pipes were delivered to us on site in lorry loads. We all helped to unload the pipes by manually picking them up, six at a time, three in each hand. Sometimes, they were fresh from the kilns and still warm, with a rough lip on the inside, which, after a while, removed the skin from the insides of your fingers. Wearing gloves did help until they wore through and eventually our hands hardened off anyway. Tractors had damp, tinny seats and no cabs in those days, exposing drivers to the elements, but this was a job I really enjoyed and became proficient at, working on land at Whitfield, Steel Rigg, Fourstones, Ninebanks, Slaggyford,

Kiln Pit Hill, Unthank Hall, Stagshaw, Garretshiels and many others I have long since forgotten.

It was at Ninebanks where my trailer reversing skills gave me a lucky break. I had loaded my trailer with about three tons of clay pipes and had to descend a steep gradient, lethally covered in ice. I knew that, if I approached tractor first, the heavily-loaded trailer would push the tractor and jack-knife and so I decided to reverse, letting the trailer pull the tractor. The problem was that I had to negotiate a farm gateway at the bottom and, as I got about halfway down, the whole unit began to slide on the ice, as the heavy trailer dragged the tractor backwards out of control. Fortunately, by staying calm and gently tweaking the steering, I was able to guide it safely through the gate into a level field.

Raymond with the work van and Fordson Major tractor leading out drain pipes

My work colleagues had seen what happened and commented "We thought you were going a bit fast". When we were at Garretshiels, we unearthed a huge boulder, which I recollect bulldozing to the bottom corner of the field near Dargues Burn, where it still remains and can be seen from the main road. Maybe I should have called it 'Ray's Rock'. It always seemed strange to unearth a single boulder that size and begs the question whether it has connections to the Roman remains in that area.

It was normal procedure to work through heavy rain showers but, if we had one of those days with continuous, unrelenting torrential rain and the working conditions became impossible, we could shelter in the van or in the warm engine compartment of the excavator. If, by three o'clock in the afternoon, there was no sign of the rain abating, we were allowed to go home early.

Moving sites required precise forward planning, as there was no margin for downtime. Once a moving day was identified, a low loader was hired to transport the Priestman digger and a delivery of pipes was arranged at our new location. Any failure in either of these two vital arrangements resulted in Old Bill throwing an angry tantrum. I was required to drive the tractor and trailer laden with our equipment between jobs, often thirty or forty miles, while one of the other workmen drove the work van.

The work van was an old Ford Ten with three gears and a six volt electrical system, which did not give a very good light. One dark, frosty evening on our way home through Fourstones, I failed to see a left hand bend in the road until the last minute and hit a bridge offside wall, badly bending the rigid front axle and rendering the van immobile. Poor Old Bill was not happy, especially as it took us about three hours to get home and, with no replacement vehicles available, we had to be dropped off and picked up daily by another gang for about two weeks, whilst Howard Maughan replaced the axle.

Back filling drains put heavy demands on the tractor clutch by constantly changing from forward to reverse gears, which required two replacements in my time there. On one occasion, I drove it without a clutch on the twenty-mile journey from Fourstones to Norman Wallace's garage at West Woodburn for repair. In that condition, the only way to stop was to switch off the engine or disengage the gear, which meant, without a clutch, I would not have been able to get going again, unless facing downhill and with a bit of luck, it just might start in gear. Whether by good luck or good fortune, I was able to negotiate all the road junctions en route without having to stop once and, when I got to the garage, Howard was waiting to guide me to the exact spot for him to replace the clutch. I was given a Massey Ferguson 35 as a replacement but it did not match up to the Fordson Power Major and Old Bill was not impressed.

Bill Richardson, or Old Bill as we called him, was a perfectionist in his job, which always came first, though every Saturday night we saw him all dressed up as Master of Ceremonies on the stage at Bellingham Town Hall, where he introduced each dance. I can hear him now: "Gentlemen, would you please take your partners for a modern waltz." Harold Bullock would also be there playing the double bass in the band.

By midsummer 1960, Dad found it necessary to have two vehicles on the farm and so he traded the Estate car in for a Hillman Minx saloon and a small Ford Thames van. The car was almost new with a full bench seat in the front and handbrake at the right hand side. The van was a bit tinny with only three gears and windscreen wipers that worked on a supply of air from the engine, which reduced when going up a hill, slowly bringing the wipers to a standstill. Dad had rented some pasture parks at Belsay to take extra sheep and the van was handy for carrying any paraphernalia to treat them and bring home the wool at shearing time.

I had become friendly with Jonnie Oliver of Hillcrest, or Jonnie Pop as most people knew him, a name associated with his father, Pop Oliver, who was caretaker for the detached pump house high above the village near the entrance to Woodhouse. We were good mates: we went everywhere together and had some great times at Butlin's and Blackpool. I desperately needed my own vehicle and, as cost was a deciding factor and motorcycles were forbidden by my parents, I discovered that vans were exempt from purchase tax and therefore a cheaper option.

A farm stock sale was coming up at Bardon Mill and a nearly new Austin A35 van was included in the auction. Dad bid for it on my behalf and there must have been someone else as keen as me as it made more than expected; but it was immaculate, with only four thousand miles on the clock, and I bought it anyway. I couldn't believe it! There was this shiny grey van, SHH 962, standing in a field and it was all mine! I just couldn't wait to drive it home.

That van never let me down and, with a heavy kerb stone in the back, would go anywhere, even in the severe wintry conditions that seemed to dominate our lives around that time. It still had the old-fashioned trafficator signal arms in the door pillars, which would pop out to indicate your intended direction, though a new law in 1958 replaced these with flashing indicators.

I taught Jonnie to drive in that van and loaned it to him to take his driving test. Jonnie worked for Jim Charlton in the butcher shop and had trained to butch sheep in the small licensed slaughter house at Yellow House. One evening, when I called to pick him up, he still had ten sheep to butch and I helped him. What he did then would never be allowed now: cutting their throats on a killing stool in the same building as those watching and awaiting their very own fate. It took him about ten minutes per sheep to convert them into hanging carcasses, following which he went through the meticulous process of swilling and scrubbing everything down before we could embark on our evening out.

For a short time, I played for Elsdon village football team and met Jim Heslop, who lived with his parents, James and Sarah, in the manager's house at Elsdon Colliery. Jim had a black Standard Eight and together we began joining friends at Mrs. Brown's snack bar at Bellingham most Sunday afternoons, playing the juke box for three pence a record or three for six pence and travelling further afield to Hexham where dances were held every Saturday night.

Meeting Beryl: By the time I was eighteen, Jim and I were frequenting most social outlets for people of our age. One Friday evening, I was on the door at a youth club dance, organised by Les Johnson at Woodburn Village Hall, when my wife-to-be unsuspectingly walked into my life.

Beryl Harrison was only sixteen, born and raised in a farm cottage at Belford overlooking Lindisfarne Castle and Holy Island. She is the youngest daughter of the late Nancy and Arthur Stanley Harrison formerly of Brownchesters Farm near Otterburn Mill. Her Dad was Farm Manager for Colonel Carr of Woodhill. Otterburn Mill was still working in the Sixties and it was not uncommon to see Otterburn Mill Tweed and Blankets hung out to dry on tenterhooks, a frame with hooks on which the woollen blankets were stretched and dried.

Delivering Coal: Jim Heslop was starting up a small coal business just up the hill from Elsdon Colliery. He had mentioned to me that there was a vacancy on the delivery round and I took the job, not quite realising what hard work I was letting myself in for. I was given a Bedford Seven and a half ton flat back lorry, which I had to stack with six tons of bagged coal. We charged five shillings for a hundredweight bag of small and six shillings for a bag of large, increasing these prices by one shilling in winter. The first load wasn't too bad, though some of the coal bunkers were in the most awkward places. I must have got back to the colliery at about one o' clock to find that any plans to sit down and have a leisurely lunch were quickly dispelled, as they urged me back to the hoppers for a second load and another delivery list, graciously informing me that, when I had delivered that load, I could go straight home. I thought that's twelve tons loaded and twelve tons delivered in one day. Thanks a bunch mate!

At first, I wore a leather pad to shield my back from the lumpy coal but it soon hardened off and worked without it. It was convenient for them that I lived at Woodburn and I had to be up early in the mornings to pick up Sid Johnson from Woodburn, Dick Jardine and David Brydon from Otterburn, en-route to work. On the second day, I was delivering an early morning load to Sharperton only to find, on arrival, that I had lost several bags of coal off the back and, on my return journey to find them, was greeted, to my horror, by none other than my former work mates in a work van driven by Alan Dodd, who was laughing his head off. He told me that the bags were on Skew Bridge not far from Holystone. When I arrived, the road was obliterated like a bomb site with coal everywhere. It must have taken me an hour to bag it up again and hump the bags back on to the wagon, though I finally got a helping hand from a sympathetic council worker. Even though this made me late back to the colliery, there was no such sympathy there as they afforded me priority over other waiting trucks and threw another six tons of bagged coal on to the wagon, sending me on my way to another village with yet another list.

I slept well that night. In fact, I could sleep for England in those days and would have slept-in many mornings, had it not been for Dad. It got to the stage when he would call me three times in a morning and I began to rely on the third call before I got up, often racing out of the house without breakfast.

I asked Beryl to join me one Saturday morning on my round but to bear in mind that this was a coal wagon and not to wear anything too light coloured. To my surprise, she appeared in a pair of white jeans, which resembled a darker shade of black when we returned. One snowy evening, I had taken Dave Brydon with me on my rounds at Sharperton and, thinking we would be okay on the hills with a load of coal on board, ventured down the hill to The Peels, only to discover that we couldn't get back up. I asked a farmer if he would tow me up the hill with his tractor but he didn't want to know. He did let us ring the depot, however, and a rescue team came out with chains for the wagon, which got us home, albeit quite late. I had arranged to meet Beryl for a Dance at Otterburn that night but phoned to say I couldn't make it.

Strangely enough, and as tough as the job was, I was enjoying being my own boss, driving to the surrounding farms and villages and meeting lots of different people. I worked five and a half days a week, delivering eleven loads, which equate to sixty-six tons a week stacked on the wagon and sixty-six tons delivered to the door. Another way of putting it is that each bag weighed one hundredweight and at twenty hundredweights to the ton, that equals one hundred and twenty bags per load – a total of 1,320 bags loaded and 1,320 bags delivered per week.

A year later, they bought me a brand new wagon, a state of the art flat-fronted Bedford TK. My boss arranged for me to meet him one Sunday morning at the top of Greenhead Bank, near Gilsland, so that we could swap over the wagons. The new one was a dream to drive and I remember driving the longer route home via Hexham for the sheer pleasure of it. But the job became no easier. The pay was good but it was an unrelenting strenuous and dirty job, a downside of which was little time for meal breaks, the absence of public toilets – and the need to have a bath every night!

There was always plenty of hot water at home but, as the house was so cold, I never wanted to get out and often fell asleep in the bath until, of course, the water temperature became unbearably cold. I was working with coal bags that were often wet, frozen or covered in snow and, by late 1962 and early 1963, the job was beginning to lose its appeal. Early one snowy morning, I was delivering coal to Rattenraw Farm when I came across a huge snow drift, completely blocking the single farm track. I had travelled so far along that it would have been risky and quite difficult to reverse all the way back to the main road and so my only option was to grab a shovel and clear the snow drift. That, I think, was the final straw. When I gave my notice, they tried to bribe me with extra pay but I had made up my mind. I'd had enough and was leaving. Hedley Scott from Otterburn took over the job. The colliery closed in 1972 and new houses now occupy the colliery site including the house Jim Heslop lived in.

Driving for the Military: John, Beryl's brother, was, at that time, friendly with Percy Fairhurst, who was in charge of Civilian Driving at Otterburn Army Camp. He made the role sound so interesting that I applied for and got a job. They gave me an Austin Champ and assigned me to drive Major Petty, the Range Officer, wherever he wanted to go. Austin Champs were versatile vehicles with a Rolls-Royce engine, a four-wheel drive option and four forward gears with a two-way lever that gave you the same four gears in reverse.

We went on to the ranges where soldiers were practising with huge twenty-five pounders going off with deafening sounds. We had no ear protection and maybe that's why I'm now so hard of hearing. Occasionally, the Range Officer would find an unexploded shell and put it in the Champ, where it rattled around behind our seats as we drove over the ranges, with me expecting it to go off any minute and him just sitting there whistling to himself!

Another side to the job was collecting visiting Senior Officers from Newcastle Railway Station in the Hillman Husky staff car but what I enjoyed most was raising the red flags around the ranges as a warning whenever live firing was going to take place. I volunteered without hesitation, especially as overtime was paid for out-of-hours call out.

It was not uncommon for me to return home quite late from a good night out, often still in drink, to find a message requesting the flags to be flown. So, instead of going to bed, I would drive to Otterburn Camp, sometimes in the middle of the night, collect my Austin Champ from the lockup garages and set off around the ranges. From there, it took about an hour to put them all up, driving out through Harbottle, Alwinton, up past Blindburn and Makendon, over the top, down past Featherwood to Redesdale Camp and finally back to Otterburn Camp.

From Christmas 1962 to early March 1963, much of the country was under snow in yet another one of the coldest UK winters on record. Main roads were only just passable but those on the ranges were completely blocked and for a number of days. I was unable to get my van up our farm road, having to leave it on the side of the main road above Woodhouse. Occasionally, I would find that the overnight frost had seized all the door locks but I had my own method of thawing them out. And it always worked!

We had snow chains fitted from time to time on the farm car but they often became slack and fell off. Town and Country tyres, which had treads like those on Land Rovers, were quite popular and we had them fitted on the back wheels but even they were not a complete solution for the snowy, slippery road conditions up to the farm. We got our own snow plough to fit on the back of the tractor, which was quite successful but it did mean travelling in reverse and you soon got a stiff neck.

Whether going north or south out of West Woodburn, it is necessary to climb a steep hill. One snowy weekend, cars were slowly skidding to a halt and so Andrew and I played Good Samaritans and towed some of them to the top with our tractor. We later learned that one grateful motorist had, on his return journey, left two double whiskies for us on the bar at the Bay Horse – but, when we failed to show up, the locals drank them. Getting up the snow-bound Long Bank on the way back from Otterburn required a fast approach and, if you didn't quite make it first time, you had to reverse all the way down and try again until you eventually made it to the top.

Back to the Farm: There was a lot of sitting about waiting for driving jobs, so I left after only six months and went back to work for my Dad on the farm in the Spring of 1963.

May and June saw the beginning of the hay season again and the bale sledge had become popular. This was a simple device, towed behind the baler and gathering about eight to ten bales, which could be released together by pulling a rope attached to the tractor.

Depositing the bales collectively rather than separately all over a field made easier work when collecting to transport home. Dad also hired me out for a week to Jim Charlton to plough some rugged open fell ground at Whiteside near the old Tone Inn with a deep-rutting, single-furrow plough. His Massey Ferguson 35 tractor was just skidding and not quite up to the job. So I drove back home and swapped the plough on to our grey Fergie, which had the larger 12-inch sized rear tyres, commanding a better grip on the rough terrain and making easy work of it.

On the day I was due to finish the job, Dad dropped me off so that I was not lumbered with a car and the tractor but, as fate would have it, I got a puncture in one of the front wheels. Being isolated, however, with no other means of transport or communication, I finished the job and drove back to Norman Wallace's garage with a flat tyre, which surprisingly survived the mistreatment.

In quieter times, I took on the role of cutting and spraying thistles. The rough ground of High Leam provided ideal conditions for wild thistles, which seemed to multiply each year and, as cutting was only a temporary solution, spraying became a more permanent alternative.

1963 Raymond with the Ferguson tractor spraying thistles

On 31st August 1963, I was best man at the marriage of my brother Andrew to Marjorie Young, a farmer's daughter and local Post Girl from Sharperton Edge. The wedding took place at Harbottle Church and the reception was held in The Salmon Inn, Holystone, a delightful pub long since closed. As there was no available housing for the newly married couple at High Leam, Andrew secured employment at Make Me Rich Farm, Capheaton, which had a house provided.

Now that I was working on the farm with two vehicles to choose from, there was no further need for my A35 van, which I sold to Andrew. That van had so many good memories for me that it was like cutting off my right arm and, for a while, I felt like I had lost my best friend. Andrew traded it in shortly after for a Ford Anglia saloon and Dad and I decided to trade in the Farm van for a Morris 1000 pickup. We spotted one advertised in a garage in Bishop Auckland and so Dad and I drove there to see it. It was in good condition and we bought it there and then.

PART 9   Changing direction 1963+

In the months following my brother's wedding, I became increasingly unsettled with the quiet, distant, almost lonely life of hill farming. Working on so many different jobs in varying environments and having frequent contact with the general public had made me aware just how isolated we were at High Leam. My farming knowledge had not progressed due to outside employment. I was twenty-one years of age and engaged to be married to Beryl and it dawned on me that, although I had worked in different occupations, I had not served an apprenticeship in any of them. I had become a bit of a rolling stone gathering no moss. Beryl and I would need a secure future and a home to call our own.

On 15th March 1965, therefore, at the age of twenty-two and a half years, I left High Leam to join the Her Majesty's Police. Height restrictions were a factor at that time and, in my case, West Riding Constabulary was the most accommodating. Andrew returned to work at High Leam, which, in December that year, was sold to the Murrays of

Cold Town, as my parents began a new venture on an arable farm near Morpeth. Jack and Nancy Wood secured work at Ravenscleugh near Elsdon but remained good friends with my parents for the rest of their lives.

On 25th June 1966, Beryl and I married at Otterburn Methodist Church, followed by a fitting reception held in the Percy Arms Hotel, and, just one week after our wedding, we packed our wedding presents and personal belongings and set off, with some apprehension, to begin a new life together in the West Riding of Yorkshire, she as a state registered nurse and I as a police constable.

Our careers proved hugely successful over the next three or four decades, both securing promotions and a comfortable lifestyle. We are now happily retired in our family home near Wakefield, discovering new adventures, socialising and meeting with our married son and two daughters and, of course, our three precious grandchildren.

When I recall my years in Redesdale, I think of the friendliness of the local people and the spacious, rolling countryside, which is in contrast with the many, heavily populated industrial and residential areas of West Yorkshire. Farming remains in my system, however, and I haven't forgotten my roots in Northumberland. In some respects, I have missed the freedom of a life in the countryside and I still reflect on the wonderful times I had growing up in that area and the local characters I had the pleasure of meeting during my teenage years and various employments. In 2009, I was privileged to take a nostalgic trip down memory lane when I was invited to re-visit High Leam, which rekindled my thoughts and left an everlasting memory of the first twenty-two and a half years of my life. Indeed, the Roman milestone from High Leam cart shed, which now stands proudly alongside the A68 trunk road above West Woodburn, serves as a lasting reminder of those early years.